GOOD TEACHERS ARE THIEVES

Tips and Strategies for Secondary Teachers on Stealing Well and Sharing the Loot

BY

WYNNE LOVE

ISBN: 098951630X
ISBN-13: 9780989516303
Library of Congress Control Number: 2013908649

Casper Books San Diego California

dedicated to
teachers
everywhere

dedicated to
teachers
everywhere

TABLE OF CONTENTS

INTRODUCTION

There is no shortage of books out there on the teaching profession. When I started out, however, I found the number of resources that had practical, day-to-day, real-life tips were few, especially for us middle and high school teachers. Having just come out of my licensure program, I was tired of spending time on theory and was eager to find some practical tips that would help me get my classroom up and running quickly and keep it running smoothly.

Once in the classroom, I was thrilled to have so many expert practitioners around me and began "stealing" all the good ideas I could. So yes—I am a thief. But when I say "teachers are thieves," I mean it in the kindest way. The best of us are masters of thieving—and sharing—all the great stuff we can find. It's thrilling that many websites are now making this a lucrative endeavor, but you'll see there are still vast amounts of free ideas out there, ready for the taking.

Now, after more than a decade of teaching—and stealing— and a few years of training new teachers, I've written the book I'd been wanting: a practical primer of the fundamental systems and strategies that will make teaching effective and fun. I've learned that I can now steal or buy all the great lessons I want, but the basic tenets were hard-earned through experience, and it's those I share here in the hopes of saving you some of that trouble. In my efforts to keep teaching a manageable profession—rather than the eighty-plus hour-a-week job it can so easily become—I have found myself coming back again and again to my "founding principles." In them I find ways to manage the workload while still teaching effectively and making decisions out of a grounded philosophy rather than desperate necessity.

Good Teachers Are Thieves sums up these principles in four main areas of teaching in so many chapters: starting the year, lesson planning, classroom management, and grading and assessment. I offer my advice on the most crucial elements for creating a successful and sustainable practice, along with suggestions for compiling and cultivating your own toolbox of strategies for the years to come.

The beauty of teaching is that it allows so much autonomy within a structured framework. This book is a guide for exercising that freedom within your prescribed duties. Since your teaching style will be unique to you and each class will have its own personality, only you can determine what will work for your classroom. Just as in parenting, however, there are strategies that work for most everyone and systems that are shown time and again to improve student achievement and success. So while each teacher and each student is unique, we are all subject to the same laws. Once those are mastered, we can be our own best resource and start creating, stealing, and refining strategies to help our students thrive.

1

STARTING SMART

JOB 1: KNOW YOUR CONTENT

JOB 2: MAKE A SCHEDULE

JOB 3: VISUALIZE YOUR CLASSROOM

JOB 4: PREPARE YOUR SYLLABUS

- Rules of Conduct
- Expectations for Class
- Classroom Procedures
- Materials
- Grading
- Calendar
- How to Reach You
- Parent Letter
- Syllabus Quiz

JOB 5: SET UP YOUR CLASSROOM

- The Physical Classroom
- Where to Keep *Your* Stuff
- Knowing the Ropes Means Knowing the School

Congratulations. You have your teaching credential (or nearly so), you have a job (or will soon), and you may even know what classes you'll be teaching. Where do you start? Below are seven key areas of preparation.

JOB 1: KNOW YOUR CONTENT

Obtain a copy of the **state standards** for your content area. Get your **textbook** and **resource materials**, and read them over. Consult your fellow teachers and ask them what they teach, what they leave out, and why. Ask which units take longest to teach or are most difficult for students and which are most important and why.

JOB 2: MAKE A SCHEDULE

Consult your colleagues and your school calendar to **make a rough sketch** of what content you'll teach during what weeks. This will be a work in progress, but at least you'll have a rough idea. I make a complete semester grid, week by week, on the computer, and update it with notes as the year progresses, so that the next year I know what really worked and why. (See sample schedule in chapter 3, "Smart Planning.")

JOB 3: VISUALIZE YOUR CLASSROOM

Hopefully you know the physical space in which you'll be working, but even if you don't, visualize your classroom. This is helpful because the physical environment itself is not as important as what you hope to see occurring within it. Are you comfortable with students in rows facing the board, or would you rather they sit in a circle, a U, or in groups? Do the desks and the amount of space in your room allow for this? How you **set up the physical space** will depend on how you hope students will work in it. This is where a lack of experience can make the job harder, so pick what is most comfortable. You can always change later. Here are questions to get you thinking:

Questions for Classroom Setup

- ✐ What arrangements are possible? What areas need to be accessible?
- ✐ What arrangement would be most comfortable for you?
- ✐ In what types of work will students engage? What arrangement best accommodates these?
- ✐ What other activities need to take place in your room?
- ✐ Where are the information-delivery devices in your room?
- ✐ Where will you work? Will you be able to face the classroom while at your desk?
- ✐ Where will you store student tools and reference materials (texts, dictionaries, pencil sharpener, hole punch, homework bin, other reference items)?

✏ Is there a place students can go if they need to be separated from the class (disruptive behavior, makeup test)?

JOB 4: PREPARE YOUR SYLLABUS

I use the term *syllabus* loosely to include the class topics as well as classroom rules, expectations, and procedures. Whether or not you choose to start the year with this document, you still need to prepare it. It will force you to take stock and **determine what you want your classroom to look like**—literally, philosophically, and pedagogically. How will grades be calculated? Will you accept late work? What rules should be in place?

The best place to start is to **place yourself in your students'** (and their parents') shoes; think about what you'd want to know about the class, and start there. For example, I used to give an overview of the units and topics covered in the class along with the classroom info, but I found neither my students nor I referenced it much. When I put the information on a calendar, though, and included test dates, grade reporting periods, and lab topics, they found it much more compelling. So my syllabus is a list of class rules and grading procedures, with a calendar of topics and due dates.

Specifically, **students will want and need to know the following**:
✏ Course expectations/requirements (workload, big projects)
✏ Classroom procedures (cell phone use, food or drink, late work, makeup work)
✏ Rules of conduct and consequences (highlight special cases: safety, cheating, and so on)
✏ Materials needed

- Grading system
- Course content and schedule of test dates, project due dates, homework assignments (if possible)
- Teacher contact info—when and where to get help
- Parent letter

Rules of Conduct

Whether you elect to state the rules outright or have the students help you create your classroom rules, you will want a vision for where you should end up. In Benjamin Mahle's book *Power Teaching*, he recommends one rule that is simply: **"Be appropriate."** I stole that rule for use in my classroom for many reasons: (1) It puts the onus on the student to know or find out what behavior is acceptable. (2) It communicates a level of respect in its assumption that the student should know exactly what appropriate classroom behavior is at his or her age. (3) It's short and sweet and requires little explanation. You don't need to get into the details of each possible infraction and the response it would elicit.

I offer students the added rationale that **anything that interferes with the learning process** is inappropriate. That includes behavior that interferes with a student's own learning (not paying attention, not bringing needed materials to class, not completing homework, cheating, plagiarism), with others' abilities to learn (talking during class, being disruptive, violating safety precautions), or with my ability to teach (distracting noises or movements, bad attitude, defiance).

> **You need only one rule: "Be appropriate."**

Then I outline the general consequences for infractions and for second and third offenses, as discussed in Chapter 2, "Smart Management."

Expectations for Class

Especially for sixth-graders, who are new to middle school, and freshman, who are new to the high school experience, some realistic expectations for the **workload** are helpful. This is tough to gauge when you're teaching any class for the first time, but you probably know if there will be multiple problem sets, lots of memorization, a few big essays, or two major projects as well as what type of daily homework the students should expect.

I paint a picture of the **type of student likely to succeed** in my class. Those students who **keep up** with assignments, **communicate** with me about their struggles, and keep a good attitude are likely to do better in my class. I also tell them about the **skills** most helpful to a student's success. For example, in my math and science classes, students don't necessarily need great math aspirations, but they do need good number sense. In the social sciences, students already know if they struggle with writing; if so, they need to plan for extra help.

Finally, it's helpful to communicate the **type of person you are** as a teacher. Some students will work well with your style and some won't. I tell my students that I have a type-A personality. I like to be in control and I tend to

> **Skills to Succeed:**
> 1. **Homework**
> 2. **Communication**
> 3. **Positive attitude**

micromanage class, meaning I will want them to be on task at all times and I will be in their face if they are not.

In my particular case, then, I begin the year telling kids that chemistry is a tough course. They'll have a significant amount of homework each day; they'll be expected to be working on chemistry at all times during class; and their grade will be based on how much chemistry they know. On the upside, I tell students that I am there to help every one of them succeed if they are willing to put in the effort, that the greatest determining factors for success in my class are conscientious completion of homework and communicating regularly with me, and that the ultimate reward, of course, is that they'll get to learn a bunch of cool chemistry!

This may seem like a **lot to cover** in the first days and weeks of class, but most of this can be communicated in fifteen or twenty minutes. It looks like more because it represents all the time and effort you've put into determining these policies. But now that you have put in all that effort, you not only have it in writing, you have a thorough rationale that will allow you to communicate the information succinctly and consistently throughout the year.

Classroom Procedures

I admit I find it a bit boring (just as my students often do) going over classroom procedures, and yet it's true that neglecting these basics can be disastrous down the road, so I **pare down the list to the essentials**. For me, these are homework procedures (when due, where to submit, how graded), seating expectations (whether they can move around, when they can use the bathroom), classroom supplies (which they can use and when, and where in the classroom is off-limits), and lab issues (unique to science, but you may have a reading area or comparable corollary: no rolling in the wheeled lab chairs, no messing with lab equipment, safety goggles are mandatory, and so on). These items will give you time to teach, which is why having them in writing and completing a cooperative syllabus quiz is a great way to go. Completing the quiz cooperatively is especially satisfying to watch because you see a classroom of students, in groups of three, earnestly discussing the policies and procedures of class and coming to consensus on the most appropriate behaviors.

> **Procedures: laid out in syllabus/class guidelines,**
> **then (cooperative) quiz at end of week**

Materials

There are always some specifics you need for your class. I mention basics like paper and pencil once in passing as a no-brainer. And, as with my one "Be appropriate" rule, I let them know I expect them to **come prepared with the appropriate materials** for the course. Coming unprepared is an action that I take as **a message that they are not coming to class ready to learn**.

Grading

Of course students want to know what they'll have to do to get the grade. This is **easy to communicate, but again, not neces-**

sarily so easy to determine on your part. I discuss philosophies of grading in chapter 4, but with respect to the syllabus, you'll want to communicate the weighting of grades, if any (how important are tests vs. homework vs. projects, and so on) how often grades are calculated and communicated, and any important specifics, such as how different types of work will be graded, what special projects to expect, and so on.

It is also important to **address makeup and late work** here, as well as other indiscretions, such as cheating and plagiarism. Will you accept late work and for how much credit? How will you handle makeup work and tests? With cheating and plagiarism getting easier to do, I like to have a statement in writing about the gravity of these infractions and the severe consequences they will incur.

Calendar

I have found that an actual **calendar of events** is more helpful than a list of topics to be taught, so I include my semester grid in my syllabus (see Chapter 3, Smart Planning). This calendar actually started out as a reference for me, but it soon became clear it would be of use to my students as well. It forces me to recognize how holidays and staff development days will encroach on the time allotted for instruction and the timing of tests and other project due dates. This is all helpful for students and parents as well, and if you're not terribly confident that you can stick to the schedule (understandably), simply acknowledge that in a disclaimer and make a point of letting students know that there will be changes. Maintaining an updated calendar online will allow all students to stay apprised of changes.

How to Reach You

Your contact information is important **for parents and students**. Let them know the following:

- all the ways you are willing to be reached (e-mail? cell phone? home phone?)
- the best times to reach you (after school hours, prep period, at school till what hour?)
- how quickly they can expect a response (within twenty-four hours? Will you return calls at the same time each day?)
- where else they can get help (other students, tutoring services, other teachers, helpful websites)

Parent Letter

It may seem a bit much, but it is becoming standard, due to the inevitable disagreements that will occur, to have the parents *and* students sign a letter acknowledging receipt of and willingness to abide by the classroom policies and procedures. This is most necessary with regard to things like late and makeup work, your grading system, and your disciplinary policies. I send a separate letter with information about semester projects as well, since plagiarism has become so rampant, and I have a separate contract about safety policies in the lab.

While this may feel cumbersome, it makes perfect sense to ensure that the students and parents have all had a chance to see what your class is about, ask any questions they might have, and agree to those policies, so that you **all start on the same page**. I also like the idea that giving your word should mean something. If they sign, as it says on my letter, **they are agreeing to follow those policies in letter** *and in spirit*.

I have rarely had to use these letters when a dispute occurs, but that may be due to the fact that they exist. Since students and parents were informed ahead of time about these policies, they are rarely challenged. Once, when a parent insisted she was not aware of the policies, it became apparent that the student had forged her signature on the start-of-year syllabus, which was something the parent was glad to have discovered!

I also like to use the parent letter as an opportunity to get the most reliable **contact information from the parents** (since my students aren't always eager to supply it) and to communicate directly with them my expectations for the course, when and how they should expect to hear from me, and some of the key strategies I have in place for keeping their kids on track, including the online grading program and class website.

Syllabus Quiz

A quiz on the syllabus is a great way **to get students talking and questioning the policies and to hold them accountable** for the information about your class without having to take the first full week of already over-planned class time to discuss the basics. As I mentioned, I like to have students complete it cooperatively, so they have the opportunity to discuss and question the policies. To facilitate this discussion, the quiz should be short and full of open-ended, thought-provoking questions that highlight the most important aspects of class.

JOB 5: SET UP YOUR CLASSROOM

The Physical Classroom

The layout of your classroom is one of the most fundamental influences on your instruction and classroom environment. Unfortunately, it is often one of the aspects least under your control. Sometimes you share your classroom with another teacher; sometimes the classroom layout or the type of desks you're given provide for only a few possibilities. With that in mind, return to your fundamental mantra: **what arrangement will be most conducive to student learning?**

The arrangement that helps your students learn best depends on your **teaching style** and on what type of work they will do most often. If you spend a lot of time in whole-class, direct instruction, you're probably best keeping students in traditional rows. If you have the students engaging in pair and group work, you may want desks paired or in groups of three or four. If you encourage a lot of class discussion, you may want a circle or U-shaped arrangement.

Most likely, your instruction will incorporate many of these strategies. The answer is to have **one standard setup with alternative arrangements** into which the students can quickly rearrange. This takes time and practice, but it's worth it.

My preferred seating arrangement is desks in groups of three. (Groups of three provide more flexibility than pairs and are more manageable than quads.) But there is only one location in my classroom where I can deliver whole-class instruction. Also, the lab tables along the outer edges of the classroom and the desks (chairs with desks attached, which can be entered from only one side) make nontraditional arrangements difficult. As a result, rows it is. But I often ask students to move their desks to accommodate pair or group work, and sometimes students arrive to find the desks in a U-shape to accommodate discussion that day. (It's always nice to keep the students on their toes.)

I must say unabashedly that I strongly recommend **assigning seats** from the start and keeping it that way. Students learn quickly that I am in control, that this is a place of learning and not a time to chat, and that they will be required to work with people of all learning styles and skill levels. I mix the students by gender, ability, ethnicity, English-language ability, socioeconomic status, and preference.

In the first weeks, I identify kids who have special needs. They often spend more time toward the front, but I try to "play fair" and give every student a chance in the front *and* the back. Nonetheless, life isn't fair, and I am frank with my students about the fact that those who will benefit most (in any fashion—discipline or content) will spend more time at the front. Students who can hack it in the back of class end up there more often. While this is not fair, hopefully they can take it as a compliment. **I try to be equitable, but my goal is successful teaching and learning for *all* students.** Since they are not all the same, I do not treat them all the same.

The difficulties posed by having students in the back of the class highlight an advantage to nontraditional seating: there is no back of the class. If students are in groups or a U-shaped arrangement, and you are circulating often throughout the class, they are less likely to feel like they're in "the back," where they are distant or forgotten. So keeping kids out of the traditional row arrangement may offer this added benefit.

Be aware of your own strengths and tendencies. A weakness of mine is that I still feel somewhat "attached" to the front of the room. Really moving through the class can require a lot of effort and practice before it becomes a habit.

Where to Keep *Your* Stuff

As you set up the student side of the classroom, you also need to set up your space. Consider the following:

- ✏ What supplies will you need, and where will you put them? (books, projector, SMART board or white board, pens and pencils, pencil sharpener, hole punch, wastebaskets, dictionaries, reference books, homework bins, student work folders, bathroom passes, and so on)
- ✏ Where will you keep your materials for that day's lessons?
- ✏ Where is your phone, and where can you put a contact list nearby?
- ✏ Where will you put your supplies and planners?
- ✏ Where will you keep your reference materials (textbooks, planning binders, and so on)?
- ✏ Where will you keep your office supplies (books, manipulatives, future lesson items, extra projector bulbs or printer ink, writing utensils, and so on)?
- ✏ Where will you keep daily-use items, like class rosters and seating charts?
- ✏ Where will you keep daily-use items that are private or need to be kept for legal purposes (attendance records, grades, family contact info, parent communication notes)?

- ✏ Where will you keep school forms? (tardy slips, referral forms, hall passes, and so on)
- ✏ Where will you work on your computer and keep related disks, thumb drives, printer paper, and so on?
- ✏ Where will you spend your time planning?
- ✏ Where will you grade papers?
- ✏ Where will you sit or stand while teaching?
- ✏ Will you have a sound system in the room? Where will it go, and how will you access it?
- ✏ Where will you keep your lunch and other personal items (wallet, keys, and so on)?
- ✏ Where is your emergency exit and where will kids go during drills?

My recommendations:

Pick a spot for your desk and computer where you can still see the class, so if you care to steal a moment to enter attendance or check a grade, e-mail, or lesson plan during class, you can do so without turning your back to the class. **I make my desk off-limits** to students so I can trust that my things won't be moved inadvertently. Have presentation materials ready, and make them all as wireless as possible so that you can keep proximity to the students while presenting material.

Have a place where you can lock your tests, purse, and other personal items, and have a spot for all your office supplies, like white-board markers, tape, extra printer ink, and so on. Have a classroom area where you have supplies available to students, like a stapler and three-hole punch, wastebasket, dictionaries, and so on. Have a spot (or better yet, a website) where absent students can see what they missed and get the appropriate handouts, without having to take time away from the class. And have a place where you put your ongoing supplies and projects: copies to be made, handouts to be used, supplies for the day's lesson, and so on.

Finally, have one binder where you keep your most important and day-to-day materials: attendance sheets, seating charts, grading sheets, your day's lesson plan, contact numbers, and so on. **This is what you'll provide a substitute when you have to be out.**

Keep a separate binder (which can be locked up as well) for ongoing documentation of students' progress, disciplinary issues, and special services. Lastly, keep your lesson plans for the entire semester or year in binders you can access easily each week as you plan the next one. (More on this in chapter 3, "Smart Planning.")

Knowing the Ropes Means Knowing the School

I cannot overstress the peace of mind it gives to know the right person to call in any situation. Similarly, **knowing your options for discipline** (what form to use and where to send kids) **can be the first and most powerful step in never having to do so.** So make it your business to get to know everyone's role in the school and what support your administration offers for discipline problems. For instance, if a burning question comes up in the middle of class, you can address it immediately if you know you can call the media center staff. You'll also know if they allow students to visit during class to pick up materials or find the answer to that question, what kind of pass they'd like to see, and whether they'd like a call ahead.

Consider the following questions and start a contact list, building your arsenal of support so you can rest easy in any situation. Your front office will have a general contact list they can give you as a starting point. Better yet, ask a colleague and steal their list!

- What **forms** do you use for what? Which should you have on hand, and how do you fill out each properly? (tardy slips, attendance, referrals, detentions, parent contact, supply recs, and so on)

- What kind of leeway do you have in issuing various forms? Can you give your own detention in your classroom? Can you forgive a tardy at your discretion or require after-school time instead of writing it up?

- How does the school/department prefer you handle student **bathroom passes**? Where are the student bathrooms, and how long should it realistically take students to get there?

- Under what circumstances is it acceptable to send a student to the office for disciplinary reasons, and what should be sent with them? Ideally, do you call for an escort? If so, whom do you call? If not, how will you know when the student reaches the office?

- What are the various **purviews of the office** staff? What types of problems are handled by which administrators (does one handle one part of the alphabet, or one group of teachers, and so on)?

- Who "holds the key" literally and figuratively to the supplies?

- What **keys** open what doors? Will you be able to access your classroom during off hours?

- Where is your **mailbox**?

- Whom do you call if you have an urgent **supply issue** (your projector bulb goes out)?

- Whom do you call if you have an urgent **technical problem** (computer goes down)?

- Who is it best to **call in case of an emergency** (lockdown situation, violent student, student in a seizure, acid spill, and so on)? Is it best to dial straight to 911, and do you need to get an outside line first? Should you call the main office first or someone else?

- Whom do you call if you have a **safety issue** or an accident in the class that is not urgent (spilled drink, carpeting repair, and so on)?

- To whom do you speak about needed **supplies**, ranging from copy paper to a new student desk to cleaning supplies to a computer monitor repair?

- Whom do you call with **computer questions** or concerns? Who are the experts in residence you could call with a grading-program or word-processing question? Who knows the e-mail system inside and out? Whom would you call if you have computer problems (printer won't print, lost computer file, and so on)?

- Whom can you consult if the **copier** fails?

- How early and late can you **access the school** outside of business hours, and how would you do so?

- Who are the **counselors**, what do they do for students, how often do they meet, and how can you find out which student is assigned to which counselor? When might it be appropriate to refer a student to his or her counselor if you suspect a problem?

- How will you get important information? When are **faculty meetings**? What are the procedures if you have to miss one? How will you be notified about test dates, pep rallies, and other class interruptions?

- Who is the school **nurse**, how qualified is he or she, and what are the proper procedures for sending students there?

- What types of student **support staff** will be working with you and your students (school psychologists, reading specialists, speech pathologists, special education teachers, and so on), and how will you know which students will receive these services and when?

- Who are the **maintenance staff** for your room, and when are they on campus? When do they generally clean your room, what can you realistically expect them to do, and how can you help them?

As is undoubtedly becoming clear, it behooves you to **get to know as many of the support staff as possible**, since they can make your life easier in so many ways. I try to know what systems are in place and why, and then follow them, knowing that the golden rule always applies and the more helpful I can be and the easier I can make their lives, the more helpful they'll be and the easier they are likely to make mine.

JOB 6: PLAN THE FIRST WEEK

Content Planning and Organization

Start with a **calendar of the entire year on one page and work backward.** First, write down all the events that are mandatory and immovable, like final exam week, holidays, staff development days, and so on. Then work backward to find the most appropriate layout for each unit. You may be part of a department that has an **imposed schedule**. In that case, **embrace it** (thank them for it!) and try to find out the rationale behind the planning. Also find out how flexible (or inflexible) it is, so you can make informed decisions about the pacing of your own classes. If your department does not have a schedule for you to follow, you've always got colleagues and the textbook whose schedules you can steal. If these are little help, here are my suggestions for planning the year on your own. Schedule first:

- ✏ vacations, **holidays, staff development days, pep rallies**, sports events, field trips, senior-class events, and other activities that affect the amount of class time you have.

- ✏ spring **testing dates**. These will affect normal class schedules and how many students may be present in class at those times.

- ✏ **projects** for which you'll need **library time, computer lab time**, or other special equipment or arrangements that may well have to be coordinated around the school schedule and other teachers.

- ✏ time needed for **final exams** and review time (if any) preceding these and special labs, papers, or other projects that will require class work time, **class presentation time or conferences**, or simply savvy due-date scheduling so as to allow you time to grade all work before semester end.

- ✏ **time to go over tests**. Without this, students get the message that tests serve as a final closure and not as part of the continued learning experience. It is hard to make time for test review, but it is worth it.

➥ **the curriculum.** Now that you see how much time you really have, you can schedule the actual content lessons as best you're able.

With day-to-day planning, follow the KISS rule: Keep it simple, sweetie. For example, many teachers **simply do the math**: there are thirty-six weeks in the year and eighteen chapters in the book; that means two weeks per chapter, starting with chapter 1 and ending with chapter 18. This is not my ideal method, but I do admire its simplicity. With a lab and test per chapter, and about four sections per chapter, that means an average of about two days per section. With allowance for some give-and-take within that structure, it certainly provides a clear template and makes for easy planning. Here are some additional tips.

➥ **Overplan**. It's always better to have too much to do than too little. Plan plenty to do, **but assume things will take longer than you think**, and be prepared to leave things out.

➥ While overplanning is great, it's easy to run long. **Plan an extra day in your schedule** for review, time for a project, or catch-up time.

➥ Plan time for taking and **going over tests** and labs, reviewing for finals, and so on. These are invariably the only times some of your students are fully motivated, and you want to be able to take advantage of it.

The First Week

Now for the nitty-gritty of the very first week—and for some soul-searching. What

> **KISS**
> **Keep it simple, sweetie.**

do you want to accomplish that first week? What tone do you want to set? How much of the logistics and procedures can you cover and still keep students engaged?

During my first week, I want students to be engaged in the class content, to know the class expectations and procedures, and to have begun to get to know one another and me. Here's how I accomplish those goals:

The First Day

For our fifty-minute period, I start with the following in place: my name and the class written on the board along with the day's agenda and objectives, the seating chart displayed on the board, and a student-information sheet and a copy of the syllabus at each desk (or handed to each student as he or she enters).

My agenda is as follows:

- ✏ Find seats and complete student information sheet (five minutes).
- ✏ Make introductions and highlight basic procedures (five minutes).
- ✏ Introduce the lab, lab groups, and our "Safety Song" (ten minutes).
- ✏ Conduct the lab (twenty-five minutes).
- ✏ Closure (five minutes).

So you see what I've done? I get the class information distributed and leave it to the students to read and learn it. I learn their names and basic information about them, and introduce them to safety and class procedures without taking the time for lengthy introductions or discussions. Best of all, I get them out of their seats and into the lab the first day.

Introductions. I greet every student as they enter every day. I also make a point of checking if I've interacted with each student each day. For this first day, I circulate constantly, repeating student names so that I can learn them all by the end of the first class. Once they are seated and I've taken roll, I give a brief bio about myself and describe the basics about the class, what they have in front of them, and what they can expect. I want them to have a chance to introduce themselves, but in the interest of not doing the typical first-day things, we leave that for the second week. In this way, the lab serves as our initial icebreaker.

I start right in, making sure they are processing everything by making use of pair-shares (where students turn to a neighbor and share what they've learned, ask or answer a question, or discuss a prompt). After telling them the most important factors for success in class (conscientious homework completion, communication, positive attitude), I have them turn to a neighbor, introduce themselves, and tell each other these three things. Note that this can turn into a ten-minute process, and I've only allotted myself five minutes here, so I watch my schedule closely.

Basic procedures and the student information sheet. I start by asking the students about themselves: their name and contact info, how they feel about school (their strengths and weaknesses), and what else they enjoy doing. These days, I have this online for students to complete electronically, but they have a hard copy (or it's on the board) as class starts, so they can prepare their answers while I meet and greet. Whether they complete this on paper or online, it is a must; to help them succeed, I must have their contact info and any relevant information I should know about them.

Agenda and objectives. For my own sake and theirs, I post the daily agenda and objectives. I point these out and go over them explicitly. We accomplish the first two immediately. These are the objectives for day 1:

"By the end of class today, you will be able to...

1. Name four people sitting near you.
2. Tell three skills that will help you succeed in chemistry.
3. Recite the "Safety Song."
4. Give an accurate explanation for the Rainbow Lab."

Safety discussion. This discussion happens under the guise of introducing the lab. I announce that we will discuss all safety rules and regulations of lab work eventually, but that the number-one cautionary procedure is lab goggles. I model them, explain about the song celebration that occurs in the wake of any infractions (see "Safety Song" below), and tell them a few important details about the lab itself.

The Safety Song (sung to the tune of "You Are My Sunshine")

I love my goggles, my safety goggles.

They keep me safe when we're in the lab.

They help protect us and even look cool.

Please let me wear my goggles all day.

It is goofy for sure, but it keeps things light-hearted, while still making the point that I expect them to wear them at all times with a positive attitude.

The Rainbow Lab. This is a great beginner lab for most any science class. Students are asked to work in trios to pipette exactly 3 ml of three different salt-water solutions (colored red, yellow, and blue) into a 10 ml graduated cylinder, with the cleanest division possible between the solutions. The trick, they learn, is to learn quickly that the solutions have different densities, so they need to place them in the right order, densest to least dense, in order to make and maintain the clearest end product. What I like is that it involves some abstract science concepts (density can be a tough one to master) and also stresses the importance of careful and measured lab skills, since the rubric gives highest points to layers most perfectly delineated. Again, I have to run a tight ship here. It is a lot to accomplish the first day, but it's an engaging way to start the year. During the lab, I continue to circulate and learn names, provide assistance when needed, and keep things moving along. I make sure to leave five full minutes for cleaning up all lab materials and for the most-often-missed lesson element, closure.

Closure. The point of closure, as you know, is to give the students one final chance to show if they have mastered the day's objectives. I leave a slip of paper on each desk with a question they must answer. On this day, they could get any of four prompts, each of which matches one of the objectives: name four of your classroom neighbors, name three skills that will help you succeed in chemistry, explain what made the red solution "heavier," or recite the "Safety Song." It's always nice to throw in a few wild cards, so I usually have a slip or two with a question like, "Now what's your favorite class?" or "Who looked coolest in their goggles?" These sillier questions do push the boundaries of the classic "Don't smile 'til Christmas" rule (Chapter 2), but as you'll see in the upcoming section, "Attitude Adjustment," I've learned to embrace this need for levity on my part.

Getting to Know You

The balance of the week, I have **four main objectives** for me and my students:

1. **Students (and their parents) will know the rules and procedures and basic expectations for my class.** I accomplish this through the parent letter and the syllabus quiz.

2. The students and I will **get to know one another**. I accomplish this by performing one of many icebreaker activities I've collected over the years. As you'll see, I recommend **creating your own "toolbox,"** whether it's in binders, a file cabinet, or on the computer, in which you collect and save all the great ideas you find, create, beg, borrow, and steal throughout your career. I try to keep everything electronically and minimize the paper, so I have a computer folder labeled "Icebreakers," in which I've saved a variety of different activities that can serve that purpose. These include a class scavenger hunt (finding classmates with your same birthday, favorite color, and so on), a class bingo game (matching students to various attributes on your bingo card), or other more individualized activities, such as creating your own "vanity license plate" or bringing in five items that tell something about you. I vary the activity each year, picking whatever sounds fun.

3. I make it my goal the first week to **identify at-risk students**. With the information I've been given by counselors and the administration, plus whatever new information the student or his or her family provides, along with my observations in class, I can usually get a pretty good idea which students are going to need extra attention this year.

4. Finally, I **begin making positive contacts with parents**. It's always my goal to make at least one positive call to every family each semester. Sometimes I call at the start of the year just to say hello and ask if they have any questions. During the rest of the year, I make calls based on my positive observations of students. Some years I'll use a **"superstar of the week"** program, in which I pick one stu-

dent each week to reward and praise for his or her good work the past week. I start by calling home on Friday afternoon with the good news. The student then gets privileges in class the following week, like sitting in our cushy lab chairs, picking his or her partner for certain activities, being first to leave the class, and so on. I don't suppose I should be surprised at the amazing reactions I get from parents, but especially by high school, many do not hear from their child's teacher often, and they appreciate it.

Attitude Adjustment: Be Yourself

Many new teachers fall into the trap of **wanting to be liked** by their students. We all look for validation, and as new teachers we especially want to feel that we are making a difference and that the students like us, look up to us, and enjoy our class. But that yearning to feel we are making a difference can easily translate into catering to students or caving on important issues.

I used to agonize over making class fun and entertaining, but I think the smarter focus is on **what will engage the students in their** *learning*. Not only have I realized that they can like and enjoy class without lots of fun extras, I have seen that the teachers who tend to care the least about their popularity (but are passionate about their students and their job) are often the most liked.

I also have discovered that when looking for validation about my teaching, my students are often the last place I should look. They have strong opinions, and often valid ones, but you are the professional, and you are more likely to know what's good for them and their learning than they are.

So by "be yourself," I mean it is in your best interests to answer questions honestly and admit when you don't know the answer to every question. That said, I think it is still valuable to put on a confident face, even if you don't truly feel confident (yes, fake it!). For example, if they ask you point-blank if you're a first-year teacher, I'd 'fess up, but not without making the point that I've been highly trained and am well prepared to teach them.

As far as confidence goes, it has always helped me to remember that insecurity is really equivalent to self-consciousness, so **to become less insecure, we need to become less self-conscious.** That is accomplished by **focusing on the task at hand** rather on how we may appear as we do it.

Being yourself also means knowing yourself as a teacher, and that may take time. I have learned that I like joking around with my students, bringing in crazy demonstrations, and even wearing a goofy costume from time to time. I can't stay serious for long; I enjoy teaching too much. But I've also learned that I need to help my students see that my cheerful nature won't prevent me from grading harshly. One of my mentors writes in his classroom guidelines each year, "Don't mistake my jovial good nature for a lack of academic resolve." I have stolen that phrase because it fits me as well. My students see me as such a cheerful, affable person that they sometimes assume I'll forgive a late paper or understand if they aren't ready on their presentation date. When those incidents occur, and I get the inevitable look of pained incredulity at my willingness to stick to the due date, I remind my

> **"Don't mistake my jovial good nature for a lack of academic resolve."**

students of this phrase from my guidelines. I can be happy-go-lucky and still hold them to high standards.

JOB 7: DIVE IN AND HAVE FUN!

Now that you've done all the hard work of planning and preparing, remember why you got into teaching in the first place, and **go enjoy your students**. We can all take ourselves (and our jobs) too seriously. While I recommend taking your *students* seriously, I also recommend a lighthearted approach to what you do. Go easy on yourself. Don't take things personally. Know you'll make mistakes, say or do things you wish you hadn't, and plan a lesson that doesn't go well. Cut yourself some slack and work on improving just one thing at a time. Don't expect to master it all in the first year or even the first decade. Do your best for your students, steal all the great ideas you can find, take care of yourself, and roll with it.

2

SMART MANAGEMENT

JOB 1: **STAGE A GOOD OFFENSE**
- Plan a Great Lesson
- The Best Defense is a Good Offense

JOB 2: **GET TO KNOW YOUR STUDENTS**
- Know Their Names
- Observe and Inquire
- Attend School Events

JOB 3: **CULTIVATE AN ENVIRONMENT OF MUTUAL RESPECT**
- Treat Students with Respect
- Respect Yourself
- Never Lose your Cool

JOB 4: **HAVE A PLAN**
- Follow a General Disciplinary Plan
- Special Cases

JOB 5: **"DON'T SMILE TILL CHRISTMAS"**

Classroom Management

You can bury yourself in books on classroom management. Maybe that's because this is the area that seems most elusive to us, not because we're not good at it, but because it is so hard to predict the behavior of every type of student and the "perfect" response. The good news is, despite the numerous books on the subject, most overlap in the key elements that lead to the greatest success. The basic strategies you've learned, such as praise and proximity, really do work, but I find a broader philosophy can be as helpful as a lot of specific strategies. My recommendation is: get to know your students, set up clear and consistent procedures and consequences, and plan great lessons.

JOB 1: STAGE A GOOD OFFENSE

The best way to deal with management problems is to keep them from ever arising, and the surest way to ensure that is to **plan a great lesson.** That is easier said than done, but the single most important factor in keeping kids well behaved is keeping them engaged. If you plan well-structured and relevant lessons, there simply won't be as many opportunities (or as much interest) in disrupting them or losing focus. Hence, **the best defense is a good offense.** This doesn't mean your lessons need to be Vegas productions or cater solely to students' interests, but they do need to be relevant. Many behavior problems (lack of interest, lack of motivation, boredom, difficulty with the material, and so on) stem from issues that can be overcome with interesting and well-planned lessons. We cover that topic in the lesson planning chapter, so skip ahead if you like. Now on to the management skills that enhance the lesson.

JOB 2: GET TO KNOW YOUR STUDENTS

Know Their Names

There's nothing worse than wanting to get a student's attention and not knowing his or her name. **Learning students' names has to be your first priority.** It is the most fundamental skill to teaching well, even when you're a substitute. Not only does *not* knowing students' names show a lack of effort, but it shows a lack of respect as well, so learn how to pronounce those tricky names, ask how students would like to be addressed, and use this as your first step in getting to know your students well enough that you can really do them some good.

You simply can't manage a class when you can't get students' attention. If you have to use other methods or rely on other students to help out, these actions undermine your power and credibility (hence the challenges of being a substitute). So, as you saw, I repeat students' names many times in the first class period. I tell them up front that I will be staring at them a fair amount this first week and repeating their names to myself and that they should simply try to ignore (or enjoy!) that attention as best they can. Many get a kick out of my attempts to remember their names as their clothing and hairstyle changes trip me up. (Plus, you can learn a fair amount about each student as you discover whether they seem to take a sick pleasure in you getting it wrong or they try to help and correct you as kindly as possible.)

Observe and Inquire

Take a genuine interest in your students. Ask how their weekend was, inquire about their last game or recital, and most important of all, **observe your students**. I am not as good at this as many of my colleagues. They can tell immediately if something is "off" with one of their students. I am not as intuitive, so I work all the harder at checking in with each student every day and taking a moment to observe them, ask questions and really listen to the answers, and notice when things seem to be going well and when they don't.

Attend School Events

It can make a real difference to students if you make the effort to **attend some of the events in which they participate** outside of school: sports, plays, concerts, local events. Many students will be amazed you made time to attend—and extremely flattered. I am consistently surprised at the hidden talents (unknown to me, at least) that my students possess, and I certainly know them better and have a greater respect for them when I see what they enjoy and what they can do.

JOB 3: CULTIVATE AN ENVIRONMENT OF MUTUAL RESPECT

Remember that your guiding disciplinary philosophy is this: **anything that interferes with the learning process requires dis-**

ciplinary action. You know when you'll need to mete out discipline, but the trick becomes how to do it best. We've all seen examples of teachers who cannot have their authority questioned and who discipline rather indiscriminately. As I mentioned earlier, it's much better to have students who comply out of respect rather than fear.

Treat Students with Respect

You communicate respect for your students in many ways. Treating students with respect means arriving prepared and excited to teach, calling each student by name, working to help each one of them be successful, and, when disciplining, giving them the benefit of the doubt, not jumping to conclusions, and addressing them respectfully and privately.

You can easily burn a bridge with a student if you don't treat him or her respectfully, especially when correcting misbehavior. The good news is that you have a lot of options for how react to any infraction. Ideally, **communicate the issue to the student privately**. Public correction can be a valuable tool in the classroom, showing all students what is expected and using that negative feedback to keep the offending student from making the same mistake, but tread cautiously here. Here's my rule of thumb: if the infraction is one which the majority of students are already noticing (defiance, disrupting class, inappropriate public remarks), they also need to see you handling it. "Handling it" may be (and probably should be) as simple as quietly correcting the student or telling him or her you'll need to speak together privately after class. But if the behavior is truly a "teachable moment" and can be used as such without shaming the student, it may be a good opportunity to do so. Take a look at the infractions below, and decide what reaction would be most appropriate.

- A student turns to a neighboring student and tells him his shirt is "gay."
- A student shows up to class with no materials.
- A student takes a look at the assignment sheet and says loudly, "This is stupid."
- A student is texting on his or her phone during a lecture.
- A student is texting on his or her phone during a test.

How do you think you would handle each of these situations? I believe the first example is a teachable moment, because many students don't find using the term *gay* offensive and don't understand why I might. So, rather than scolding, I would thank the student for the comment. This gives me the opportunity to point out why that kind of language and tone aren't acceptable in my classroom.

In the second example, the student needs to know he or she cannot come to class unprepared. I can and should communicate this privately, but I also must communicate it immediately, since he or she can't successfully complete class without the appropriate materials. So interrupting class to pull the student aside is necessary, but it must be private, because we don't yet know why the student came unprepared—and there are many possible reasons. If it is due to a family emergency, I help the student through the day and never acknowledge it publicly. If, instead, the student simply didn't care to bring his or her work, that conversation now constitutes a student conference to address that misbehavior. But I've made a respectful and private correction, and if the rest of the class is aware, they see that the infraction was addressed promptly.

Of course I could raise my voice and scold a student openly, and she might correct the behavior to avoid such embarrassment in the future, but **I'd rather have students who do what I ask because they want to do well rather than because they fear the consequences**. In my experience, people who try to get others to do their bidding by yelling don't succeed for long. I try to earn students' respect and foster their desire to succeed by keeping my eye on the prize – that I am here to help them learn – and doing whatever it takes to fulfill that job description.

In the third example, simply ignoring the statement is very likely the best response. Responding to it gives the student an additional opportunity to make his case. Better to start the lesson and let the students decide for themselves, perhaps acknowledging subtly at the end that today's lesson might have seemed simple at first, but that they hopefully found it effective in teaching the concept at hand.

In the fourth example, all students know that texting, reading, talking, or anything other than actively listening is inappropriate (there's that word!) during instruction, so discreetly taking the phone is enough, telling the student, if you like, that they can retrieve it after class, at which time you can privately remind them of the class guidelines to which they agreed, communicate your objections, and insist it not happen again. If the student chooses to object and make the transgression public, that is their choice. Then, you give them the choice to voluntarily put it on your desk (never succumb to a wrestling match) or they suffer the next step in the discipline plan (parent phone call and detention or other logical consequence).

For the fifth example, texting during a test, the response is the same initially, but now that there is the possibility that they were cheating, you will also need to contact the parents and set up a private conference to require an oral defense of the test. (More on this below.)

Respect Yourself

In general, you can see that all of these infractions could be addressed quietly and privately, and it is only if your own sense of self-respect is at stake that making the correction more public may be helpful and worth the risk. Keep in mind that doing so is generally helpful to you, not the student, but classes do have a personality of their own, and individual students can have an impressive effect. If the student is more persuasive than you, the rest of the class needs to see you addressing his or her misbehavior. Either way, most important is that you do address it, for it is when you let it slide that you open the door to future infractions by this student and others. The key here is to **maintain your own sense of self-respect**, for it is **when you allow students to bully you that you lose the respect of the class**. If you are uncomfortable with a behavior, address it. Just be sure to do so when you can remain calm; the students need to see you calmly and confidently moving to the next step in your disciplinary plan.

Never Lose Your Cool

Conscientious students rely on you to keep the less motivated in line, and they can't help but be disappointed when you've been bested. Meanwhile, the attention-getters make note of the apparent chink in your armor. Always better to seem unflappable, and **the key to keeping your cool is simply practice**.

Parenting has been a great teacher for me in mastering my emotions. The first lesson is that it never feels good to lose it, and it is rarely an effective disciplinary strategy. Second, it takes conscious effort to avoid losing it. I have to remind myself to take a deep breath or a break before responding, that this is not personal, and to remember to focus on the behavior and not the individual. Third, turning a blind eye to misbehavior generally only invites more of it. Fourth, **I've found I am most likely to lose it when I don't feel I have an appropriate consequence**. When I don't know how to stop the behavior, I holler. If I have a consequence that fits the crime, I stay calm because I have a plan for correcting the behavior in a way that will matter to the student as well, so I can rest easy.

I learned that one the hard way, multiple times. I have (I'm sorry to admit) twice found myself in a tug of war with a student, and I recognized right away that no matter who won, I was going to look like the loser. In both cases, I realized I lost my cool because I didn't have a good consequence at the ready – I felt I was out of options. Now I make it a priority to always have a clear set of reasonable consequences that will matter to them and therefore will allow me to, hopefully, get that student and the others back on track. If I can't do that for some reason, I tell the student I will address the infraction later. Not a great result, but better than the alternative.

Hence, the importance of a good disciplinary plan that you enforce consistently. I have often found myself reluctant to buckle down and discipline certain students when what they are doing is hard to define as misbehavior or subtle and infrequent (like reading the text during other activities or asking excessive questions). But I ultimately scold myself as I realize that, despite the seemingly positive nature of their behavior, it has been disrupting my teaching or other students' learning and is driving me so crazy that when I do finally address it, I react (rather than act) and lose my cool. Certainly you need a measure of freedom and trust in the classroom (allowing students some leeway), but anything that can be justified as interfering with the learning really should be addressed to avoid it escalating or setting a bad precedent for other students.

Lastly, don't overlook the valuable resources around you. Your fellow teachers may have some great ideas on preventative measures and logical consequences. **Make time to talk to your colleagues and steal their good ideas**.

JOB 4: HAVE A PLAN

As we discussed earlier, one rule is really enough: be appropriate. But to enforce that rule, you need a plan in place. Some teachers make this a cooperative effort with the class, which is another great way to involve them and gain buy-in. Either way, a general disciplinary plan show parents and administrators that you've thought things through and it also gives you a clear, objective plan to follow when you're not sure what to do next. Of course you'll skip some steps and involve the administration immediately for infractions like drugs, alcohol, or violence, but for more minor infractions, this model should suffice.

General Consequence Model

1st infraction:	Student conference
2nd infraction:	Student conference and parent contact (phone call or e-mail home) *or* detention or other logical consequence
3rd infraction:	Student conference, parent contact, *and* detention or logical consequence; student can no longer earn the highest behavior grade on his or her report card; written referral warning is sent htome
4th infraction:	Conference with student, parent, and counselor; written referral (strike 1)
5th infraction:	Conference with student, parent, counselor, and administration; written referral (strike 2)
6th infraction:	Final referral (strike 3); student is dropped from course

So you see I start by politely and respectfully pointing out the problem behavior to the student, giving them the benefit of the doubt. The majority of students will correct their behavior after simply being pulled aside and told there's a problem. Should there be a second offense, we speak again but I also contact the parents or, if appropriate, I use a logical consequence (see below) that I have confidence will be as effective or more effective than involving the parents. The consequences escalate as shown. If the student behavior persists to the point it is consistently disrupting other students and their own learning, I need to involve the parents and administration.

The most important element of the plan is to **write everything down**. Information is power, so I keep a binder with a page for every student, and I jot down a note (or often, have the student do so,) every time we have a problem, or a success. The binder I use is the collection of student information sheets from the start of the year. I make a note on the back or just add a sticky note, so it doesn't take much time, and now I am armed with information. Telling a parent the student's cell phone is a constant distraction is much less effective than being able to show that the student has had their cell phone out in class on 9/13, 9/22, 10/1, 10/4, and 10/7.

1st infraction: Student conference. This doesn't have to be as formal as it sounds, but it does need to be documented. All that's required here is to get the student's full attention for a moment or two so that you can clearly communicate the problem. A general plan is to: 1) communicate to the student what the behavior was that was a problem, 2) explain why it was a problem, and 3) be sure they know what the consequence is for this behavior and what it will be in the future if the behavior continues.

Tip #1: I start by asking the student why they think I want to talk to them. This not only gives the student a chance to take ownership and explain or apologize, it often keeps me from sounding like I'm scolding.

Tip #2: **Focus on the behavior, not the student**, just as you have been trained to do. It's not personal, it's just a necessary correction of unhelpful behavior.

Tip #3: Write it down. **Make a note of the conversation**. For truly minor issues, you may not waste your time here, but it can be a huge help down the road if the behavior isn't corrected.

2nd infraction: Student conference and parent contact OR consequence. Why the "or"? Frankly, you could leave it out. It is always a good idea to contact the parents sooner rather than later, so you could include that in all areas of your discipline policy. But, with some behavior, you may not feel it warrants that kind of involvement, and **there's also a great deal to be said (and often an appreciation and even respect for you on the part of the student) for resolving issues between yourselves**. If you think the behavior can be stopped by another talk with the student and a detention or other logical consequence, maybe you'll elect not to include the parents. If, however, the behavior was particularly offensive, you worry it is a sign of things to come, or you suspect there isn't likely to be a change in behavior without some serious intervention, then the parent contact may be warranted as early as this second slip-up.

It's also good to "**think like a parent**." As a parent, I appreciate teachers who use their judgment to resolve issues in class without my help, but there are also incidents about which I'd want to be made aware. For instance, if my daughter has missed a homework assignment here or there, but is generally conscientious, I'd expect that the teacher is noticing and asking my daughter about it, but not contacting me. However, if my daughter cheated on a quiz, first time or not, I'd want to know about it! So in trying to determine whether to call the parent, take into account whether you think the parent would want to know, whether you'll build any bonds with the student without burning bridges with the parents if you don't call. Ultimately, **when in doubt, call**.

Tips for Contacting Parents

1. Communicate something positive first.
2. Talk about the problem behavior, not the "problem child."
3. Show parents that your call is out of concern for their child's learning.
4. Listen.
5. Describe how it can be (or already is being) resolved, and be open to hearing other suggestions or other problems that need to be addressed.
6. End on a positive note.

My conversations with parents tend to go something like this: "Jeremy has been doing a much better job on his homework completion these last two weeks. [positive feedback] He was also really excited about his soccer win over the weekend. That must have been great! [possible chit-chat] The reason I'm calling today is that I noticed that he was copying answers off a classmate's assignment before he turned it in. [explain the behavior] I've already spoken to Jeremy about this and he promises it won't happen again, but I thought you'd also want to know. [Now listen. The parents may express surprise and concern, or may explain the behavior due to his busy schedule. This information helps shed light on the student's life, motivations, and the amount of support he, and you, are getting at home. Acknowledge their concerns, thank them for their help, and make sure you communicate your plan.] I understand and I appreciate your support. My concern is that if Jeremy is copying answers he's not learning the material [concern for student's success] so when we spoke, Jeremy and I agreed that he will keep an appointment with me [detention] tomorrow to make sure he understands the material he turned in today. In the future, he knows that he can come in after school or before class if he has questions on the homework, rather than copying off another. [resolution] I know Jeremy can do the work, so I expect he will do just fine from here on out. [ending on a positive note]"

If you have these steps listed out or at least clear in your mind, it will make it easier for you to make the call and to listen to any insights the parents have to share. Remember that the point of the call is to find things you and the parents can do to help the student be more successful. Let them know you're on the student's side, but be straight as well. If the student is disrupting class and making it difficult for you and for other students, the parents need to know that. If he or she doesn't appear to be spending any time on the work outside of class, tell them that as well. Then, be ready with suggestions that can help.

Of course, most parents will be distressed to hear any kind of bad news. Some will say just what we hope for: "I'll talk to him tonight and we will make sure this won't happen again." Some will try to explain or justify the student's actions. This is also helpful as you may learn there is little opportunity at home to do homework or get help. You may realize you'll have to come up with some alternative ideas for helping them. Worst case, the parents think you are being too harsh or that your consequences are unjustified. If your goal is always to help each child be successful, your explanation should be sufficient. But I find **it never pays to argue with a parent**, and it's certainly not professional. The best strategy is to remain detached and calm, and keep bringing the conversation back to how the behavior interferes with the student's own success or the success of others in the class. If you are getting nowhere, and the parent doesn't suggest it first, **sug-**

gest that you all sit down together with one of the administrators to discuss possible resolutions. Then the parent knows they can have their say, and you know you will have an ally in the room who can help support your work, as necessary.

3rd infraction: Student conference, parent contact, and detention/consequence. Report card effort/behavior grade lowered. Referral warning given. If you reach a third infraction, you will certainly want to talk to the student and the parents at this point, especially since your plan indicates the student can no longer earn an "E" on their report card (in our district, "E" for "exceeding expectations" is the highest behavior mark). It is getting serious now, so I also make sure the student and parents know that if the problem continues, they will be "written up" with a referral to the office for further disciplinary action, and could ultimately be removed from the course.

I also impose some sort of logical consequence. It can be something generic like detention but, as you've learned in your training, it is always best if you can **make the consequence fit the crime**. Better yet, focus on finding a solution to the problem. For example, for a student who is not completing her homework, the perfect consequence is also the solution: tutorial (call it detention, if you like,) after school so they can get their homework done with your help or that of another student. If the student made a mess in the lab, or brought a soda into class which spilled, a clear related consequence would be to have them stay after to clean it up. Then don't forget to have a conversation (which is really all a conference is anyway) in which you brainstorm solutions for how the student can get help for themselves on their homework or avoid making the mess in the first place.

As for the third infraction, by the time a student is doing something wrong, especially the same thing wrong, for the third time, you are probably getting tired of addressing it. If you've had productive conversations with the student and still aren't seeing resolution, then the coddling and coaxing must end, and the student must see that you mean business. Now you make it clear to the student and parents that, if your interventions and whatever the parents have tried at home have not made the difference, **future infractions will warrant referrals to the office**.

A **"referral,"** or whatever you call them in your district, is the paper that **gets the administration involved**. Hopefully your administration is supportive and their referrals are effective; **using them sparingly** will help ensure that. As noted, you'll involve the administration much sooner for infractions like drugs, alcohol, or violence, but of course you don't want to be running to them every time you have a problem. For general behavior issues, you'll want to solve the problem yourself. But just like the parents, the administration would rather know sooner than later about students who are at risk and who may require a larger team of support to get them through, so don't hesitate to call in the big guns if you feel you need them.

All school districts will have a disciplinary plan of their own. Find out what it is. In mine, the student gets three strikes and they're out, meaning they are dropped from the class with a failing grade on their transcript and, of course, no credit for the course. Everyone is notified at the time of each referral, so I have sometimes had to swallow my frustration and resist issuing a strike 2 or 3 if the notifications about strike 1 are only just arriving. If necessary, the office should support you by visiting your class or providing another place for the student to work as you give the student time to improve their behavior.

So you are all on the same page, **this is the time when you explain the "three-strike" system and what it means to the student, and make it clear you will be making use of the system from now on if the behavior does not improve.** As always, it helps to remember that this process is about helping the student solve the problem, *not* punishing them or getting them out of your class. These are the students that need your help the most (even if they are causing trouble for the rest at times!) so they need a chance to change that behavior. The student, parents, and counselors all deserve time to work to correct the problem. Of course, some students would welcome removal from your class, but counselors and administrators should be supportive in making it clear that this is not a ticket into some other teacher's class or a route to study hall or free time either.

Keep in mind that the infractions noted in the first, second, and third strikes don't necessarily have to address the same issue. Be sure to **make it clear you're addressing the overarching problem** the student is having, such as defiance, apathy, or disruptive behavior. That way, parents and students know they are *not* getting a warning that they must stop talking during lecture, but that they must stop all behavior that disrupts class and limits your ability to teach.

4th infraction: Conference with student, parent, counselor, and administration, consequence, and referral – "strike 1." Now things are getting serious. The behavior has been addressed three times and still has not improved. Since you already warned the student and his or her parents that if the behavior continued, the administration would be getting involved, it is time to put your money where your mouth is. **For this fourth infraction, you write a referral, send the student to the office, and make it clear** (verbally and in writing) that this is their "first strike." You **talk to the student** about how to resolve the issue, **communicate with the parents** so they realize the issue has not been resolved, and **communicate with your administration** (and perhaps the counselor's office, if the issue is an academic one) so they are aware as well.

A word on the referral: Administrators, keep in mind, aren't present for whatever has transpired in the class, and yet must often be the final judge and jury of a student's fate. **Help your administrators out by documenting everything and being explicit on your referrals**. That means you quote the exact words the student used, describe the attitude and any hand gestures, etc. (Are you cringing now?!) Be careful, as always, to remain as objective and detached as possible, withholding judgmental or subjective comments, describing the behavior and not the student. The more your administration knows about the incidents, the more help and support they can give.

A note on sending students to the office: **You can send the student to the office during class or afterward, but beware of the pros and cons to both**. Sending them during class is probably an even greater disruption than the infraction itself, or at least extends the length of the disruption. Unless you've written the referral ahead of time, you will have to take the time during class to do so. Then you will have to endure the scene the student may make when you ask him or her to leave. If you think you need to make the point, to the rest of the students, that this behavior won't be tolerated, or if conducting class seems impossible with the student present, it may be worth it. If you do elect to send the student during class, have an administrator escort the student or check to make sure the student got there.

Another option is to write up the referral and hand it to them at the end of class. Then, if the student does make a scene, at least it is mitigated by the between-class shuffle. Most unintrusive, you can send the referral to the office and have the office staff summon the student out of another class later that day. This is the least confrontational method, but may not be as effective. Talk to your administration about their preferences.

5th infraction: Conference with student, parent, counselor, administration, consequence, and "strike 2." And the process continues. The trick now is determining how strict you intend to be. What misstep truly warrants another strike? Use your best judgment. You need to feel you can justify each step to parents and administrators, so the best advice is to **remain detached and objective and follow the criteria you'd been using all year long**: if the student's behavior is disruptive to the learning process, it's a problem.

6th infraction: Referral – Strike 3 – dropped from course. For students whom you simply cannot help be successful—at least at this time, in this class—every district will have a point, sixth infraction or not, where they acknowledge that this student should not continue in the class at this time. That doesn't mean they can't be successful in another class or through another program, or in this class at some later time, but they aren't capable of making the necessary changes to be successful now. Find out what options are available to you in these (rare) circumstances and what burden of proof you are expected to meet to have a student reach this threshold, but **there must be a point at which the ulti-**

mate consequence is meted out and you are allowed to run class without disruption.

You may still be getting your sea legs in this classroom management thing, but if you are making a real effort to meet student needs and have gone through the steps up to this point with a student, the sixth infraction is long enough to wait. Frankly, it is too long to wait, but it is important that every student be given his or her "due process." Why not just fail the student? You could, but **you have to keep in mind your duty to the other students.** If this one is making it harder for you to teach and for them to learn, removal may be appropriate.

Removal also has the advantage of being more tangibly final than simply failing and includes logical consequences, such as making up the credits elsewhere and finding somewhere else to be for that period. If you are to have any chance of successful classroom management, there must be a final straw, and students must be allowed to reach it. There is no defeat in that, especially as you have made the point that you are there to help students find solutions. This may be the first step in helping them; when they are ready, they can come back to you.

Special Cases

It probably goes without saying that transgressions that are flat-out illegal or put students at risk (like drugs, alcohol, violence) need to be addressed immediately by you and the administration. Some instances will be obvious, such as possession of a weapon or a fight breaking out. Others are subtle, such as substance abuse or child abuse, and you may be the eyes and ears best poised to catch them. **Keep in mind that many of the more mundane classroom management issues you face may be symptomatic of these bigger issues.**

For example, say a student actually falls asleep during class. It could be because she was up late finishing a big paper. It could also be that she is simply bored and doesn't want to make the effort (my fault and hers). She could be having problems at home that are keeping her from getting enough sleep. She could be drunk or high. Or… We could conjecture all day. You don't want to jump to the conclusion it's something wrong with your teaching, but you also don't want to jump to the conclusion that it's an unmotivated student, because there could be more going on.

This is where **your skills at listening and watching your students will allow you to learn the truth.** And don't forget, that student sees other teachers. Make use of their observations as well. Some teachers have a sixth sense about their students and are able to get to the crux of the matter in lightning speed. You may find out that they know all about what's going on with the student, or at least you'll have put another pair of eyes on the job.

Meanwhile, if you are committed to observing and getting to know your students, not only will your classroom management improve, but you'll be serving your students better because you'll see what they need and help them work through it so they can be more successful.

JOB 5: "DON'T SMILE TILL CHRISTMAS"

You've heard the expression. My cheerful nature makes this impossible, but I do subscribe to the philosophy behind it. Kids are definitely getting a feel for your limits those first weeks. If you're too permissive, it will be hard to rein them back in later. So yes, you'll want to make a point to enforce everything so students get the point that you **mean what you say**. Early on, address every infraction, including where and when to turn in homework, how to enter and exit class, talking out of turn, bathroom use, tardies, and so on. The more students see that these minor infractions are important and will have consequences (even if the consequence is simply having their mistake pointed out), the more reliably they will abide by your rules and procedures in other areas. They may still push the envelope come spring, but the effort you expend those first weeks of the year is a small price to pay for months and months of smooth sailing in the classroom.

3

SMART PLANNING

JOB 1: PLAN THE SEMESTER
- ✏ Work Backwards
- ✏ Keep it Simple

JOB 2: GET ORGANIZED
- ✏ Use Unit Binders
- ✏ Beg, Borrow, and Steal

JOB 3: MAP YOUR LESSONS
- ✏ Write <u>M</u>easurable Objectives
- ✏ Require <u>A</u>ctive Participation
- ✏ <u>P</u>rocess, Check, and Check Again

JOB 4: KEEP IT REAL
- ✏ Stick to a Schedule
- ✏ Go with the Flow

Lesson Planning

It's time to plan your year. Daunted? Don't be. If you've created your course syllabus, you already have a plan for the year. Now you'll simply lay it out in more detail.

JOB 1: PLAN THE SEMESTER

Work Backward

Just like you will for individual lesson plans, you will **start with where you want to end up** when you plan the year as well. On a school calendar, sketch in the topics your standards dictate. Then narrow it down to units, weeks, and eventually days. You already have a plan for the first few days of school, so now you make an overarching plan for the course content.

Keep It Simple

I recommend creating a calendar on the computer with a box for each day of the semester. Then use your colleagues, the textbook, and your school calendar to fill it in. Keep it simple. Even if it means a straightforward, by-the-book yearly plan, it's a start, and it's much more about how you teach and communicate each concept than it is about the order in which you do so (as long as the concepts build on each other, as necessary). It helps me to **see the entire semester on one page**, so I make a semester calendar that covers the basic topic or activity for each class (see chart, "Chemistry—Fall 2103"), and I share this with students.

The schedule is tentative, of course, but allows me to see the overall flow of the coursework over the semester, along with test dates, big projects, and final exams. It is most helpful in its ability to show how little time I have to teach all the material. It is also where I'm able to account for all the extraneous scheduling conflicts, like holidays and staff development days, that will encroach on that precious classroom time.

I write my general plan for the upcoming week on the Thursday before. Not only does this Thursday deadline keep me on top of things and at least a week ahead at all times, it also gives me enough lead time to make the copies I need. It allows me to use my planning time during the week more efficiently, because rather than juggling day-to-day and long-term planning every day, I know it will get handled on Thursday.

I write my lesson plan for each day the day before. On a given day, I have the year planned in very general terms as shown above; I have the current unit's assessments prepared and activities chosen; I have the current week's activities sketched more fully, timed out, and copies made; and I have the current day's supplies out and agenda and objectives written. I find that if I try to plan *exactly* what I'll be doing on a given day more than two days ahead, too much has changed by the time that day comes, so weekly planning happens the Thursday prior, and daily refinements happen throughout the week.

Chemistry—Fall 2013

This schedule is NOT complete. <u>Changes will be made</u> and <u>homework assignments will be added</u>. Always check the board and listen in class for changes & additions.

W Aug 21 About Chemistry & You Class Info Lab Equipment, Safety LAB: Rainbow Lab HW: Lab Notebook/ Pre-Lab! Skills Quiz! Student/ Parent Info, Periodic Table, Intro Bag, Safety & Class Contracts	Th Aug 22 Skills Inventory Feedback Student Info, Periodic Table, Notebooks HW: Safety Contract, Class Contract, Intro Bag, Periodic Table & Elements	F Aug 23 Guidelines & Safety Quizzes, Lab Recap Class Introductions HW: Book Notes & Q's 1-1 and BRING BOOK TO CLASS MONDAY!, Rainbow Lab, Periodic Table
M Aug 26 Language of Chemistry – U1HS Intro Using the Text, Taking Notes HW: Book Sections 1-2 & 2-3	T Aug 27 U1HS – 1-1&2 – Chem/ Endo-Exo demo/ Chem chgs U1HS – 1-2 - Units & Measurements, Rainbow Wrap-up LAB: Metric Mania HW: Elem 1-56, & Notes, Book Section 2-2	Th Aug 29 LAB: Wrap-up Metric Mania NOS – theory vs. law, creative science, lab work HW: Metric WS's, Book Section 1-3 & 1-4, Rainbow Lab, Pennies?
Labor Day Holiday	T Sep 7 U1HS – 1-3 – Atoms, Elements, Molecules U1HS – 1-4 – Classifying Compounds, Ions, Mixtures Pre-Labs, Start Penny Lab? HW: Book 2-1, Pre-Lab	Th Sep 9 LABS: Penny Lab? & Specific Heat Lab HW: Lab write-ups Element Tests? ??????????????????? ????????

JOB 2: GET ORGANIZED

Use Unit Binders

We all have our own systems. I suggest you look at as many colleagues' systems as you can to find one you like that you can steal and make your own. My preferred method is to keep a separate **binder for** *each unit* of my course in which I put, in order of my curriculum or text, **all the materials I may want to use**, including student consumables, teacher keys, my unit plan, unit vocabulary, reading and lecture notes, homework assignments, quizzes, labs, activities, reading materials, projects, and assessments. During a first run of any course, I put this together as I go. This allows me a quick look at all the options available to me for that unit, what is coming up next, and what content and tasks I expect students to master by the end of the unit. **These objectives for student mastery guide all my decisions as to what activities and projects should be in each unit.**

I try to have an electronic, editable version of everything in my computer files, so I minimize extra copies or reference materials in a file cabinet. Then the originals and keys come and go from the binder, bookmarked as I work through the unit. **As I go, I replace the items in the binder with my most up-to-date version and any notes on changes I should make for next year, revised timing, or how best to execute a particular lesson.** It's helpful and easy to have all my unit materials in one place (I will sometimes even copy the appropriate chapters of the text so I can highlight terms, passages, or questions, or separate pieces of them as needed within the unit). It's also satisfying to see my creations and the items I've stolen from other places (colleagues, Internet, and so on) come together to form a cohesive unit. It allows me to see the unit as whole and organize it in whatever way seems best (by standards, objectives, book sections, and so on) and to see the flow of learning (activities, lecture notes, mode of learning, and assessments for each objective).

Finally, replacing materials as I go and closing out the unit binder at the end of each unit serves as a reminder and a good incentive to replace each activity with a version that is up-to-date and ready for the next year and to make helpful notes about pitfalls and ways to make the next year's execution smoother.

Beg, Borrow, and Steal

Building my unit binder is also the perfect motivation for getting out and talking to my colleagues, checking the net, and finding the best, most engaging, most effective lesson activities and projects for helping students achieve the relevant objectives. Whether you turn to the internet, a book, or a colleague, finding (and stealing) just the lesson you need to teach that tricky standard or student is priceless. Ask those around you for their best lesson ideas and add them to your binder. Some teachers, sadly, are not inclined to share, for whatever reason, but many are delighted to be a resource to others and help spread and foster great teaching. Find them and build your arsenal of great lessons. Eventually, those binders will be a great resource you can share with others.

JOB 3: MAP YOUR LESSONS

Now for the meat of what you do: daily lesson planning. Once you're in the classroom day after day, it's not realistic or even necessary to create five- to seven-page lesson plans (like you did in your licensure program) for every lesson you teach—even the first time. But every day you *should* have a good hook or way of engaging the kids, a clear focus and measurable objective, some sort of assessment or feedback on whether the students are learning, and a moment for processing or closure to help students recognize what they've learned.

It is fairly intuitive for me now to create lessons that include all these elements, but even after many years in the classroom, **my lessons are still better if I make myself write a plan that explicitly covers each of these elements.** That's why I make a single-sheet template with space to address each of the key areas. Even if it's just a scrawl, I sketch out each of my lessons in this way.

Some lesson models are based on five fundamental elements. Madeline Hunter uses seven. Use whatever model you choose as long as it gets the job done. All of those elements are in my plan as well, but I sum it up in three general headings and call it my **"MAP."**

> M = Measureable objectives
>
> A = Active Participation (through the anticipatory set, activities, and assessments)
>
> P = Processing (through guided practice, checks for understanding, and closure)

Write **M**easureable Objectives

The logical place to start with any lesson is with the objectives you have for students. It is not only helpful but essential to have a clear idea of what you hope students will be able to do after any lesson before you execute it. **While most teachers have a clear goal, many proceed with one that is too general. Instead, you need to start with specific, measurable objectives.** Take a unit on the periodic table, for example. Your overarching goal for the unit is that students know how to read the periodic table—that is, they can figure out what it tells them and how it is organized. That's a great goal, but how will you know when a student is able to do that? What will students actually do or say that would offer sufficient evidence to show they have mastered that goal?

When I dig deep, I realize that I want students to be able to list the three key ways in which the table is organized. I also want them to be able to demonstrate this understanding by organizing elements (using unknowns) following these principles. I also want them to be able to explain why these methods of organization make sense and why they result in a table that is "periodic" and what the word *periodic* means. So it turns out there's a lot to learn, but now that I've broken it down, I can see more easily the different levels of learning expected (some of these skills fall near the bottom of Bloom's taxonomy, some near the top), and how I might best divide up the learning into separate lessons. This is why breaking the content down into specific, discrete tasks (and **writing clear, *measurable* objectives**) makes lesson planning so much easier. In short, I don't start out saying, "What will I teach?" or even "How shall I teach this?" but instead, **"What will students know and be able to do by the end of this lesson?"**

The ABCs of objectives, as described in *Models, Strategies, and Methods for Effective Teaching* by Hellmut Lang and David Evans, sum up the key elements needed in any complete objective and are a nice shorthand way of remembering the key elements: audience (A), behavior/task (B), condition/circumstances (C), and degree/extent (D). Including all these elements will surely give you a complete and thorough objective, but **the absolute key to writing useful objectives is ensuring that part B, the behavior or task, is** *measurable*. Take a look at the following objectives and decide which you think are poor and which are good.

* Introduce students to the Spanish language.
* Teach how the cell works.
* Students will understand the connection between Pearl Harbor and World War II.
* Students will be able to explain iambic pentameter.
* Students know how to use the Pythagorean theorem.

Yup, you guessed it. They're all bad. Why? They aren't clear, specific, and measurable.

The **most crucial piece to any objective is the verb**. There's a big difference between "Students will understand the connection between…" and "Students will be able to list three ways in which the attack on Pearl Harbor led to US involvement…" You know you want them to understand the subject matter; that's a nice general goal. But how will you know they understand it? How will you measure that? Once you answer that question, you realize what your objectives should really say, and you have a better idea how to help students get there. Measurable objectives make for more specific and therefore more numerous objectives, but they also make the learning goals much clearer for everyone.

The ABCs of Objectives*

A = Audience
(the student)

B = **Behavior (the measurable
activity)**

C = *Condition (the
environment/aids)*

D = <u>Degree (to what extent,
how many)</u>

Examples:

Using a map of the United States, students
will be able to **label the <u>thirteen</u> original colonies**.

With use of a calculator, students
will be able to **graph <u>five</u> parabolic equations**.

With their fellow team members, students will be able to **find and
define <u>six</u> key terms** from the current unit in the textbook.

*from *Models, Strategies, and Methods for Effective Teaching*
by Hellmut Lang and David Evans

It's more work up front, of course, but **being that specific in
your objectives** will provide laser focus for your lessons and for
your students. Even better, it **will necessarily point toward logical
activities for achieving each objective**, and it will provide a nice
way of seeing the scope of your objectives, from rote learning to
real understanding and analysis (so that you use the full scope of
Bloom's taxonomy).

So **start writing the objectives for any lesson with: "Students
will be able to..."** rather than "Students will...." **Focus on ac-**

tion verbs that are measurable, and avoid verbs that are vague or must be judged subjectively, like *explain, know,* and *appreciate.* Truth be told, I often start with those verbs, but when one shows up, I stop, think about how I'll actually know they "know," and then rewrite the objective to the more defined standard.

Here are the objectives from above, rewritten to be clear, specific, and measurable.

- ✏ "Introduce students to the Spanish language" becomes "Students will be able to list five countries in which Spanish is spoken; students will be able to count to ten in Spanish; students will be able to recite and properly conjugate the verb *hablar* for each subject."

- ✏ "Teach how the cell works" probably encompasses a number of lessons. The first day's objectives might be "Students will be able to list the four main components of an animal cell and give the purpose of each" or "Students will be able to distinguish between animal and plant cells, listing three main differences between them."

- ✏ "Students will understand the connection between Pearl Harbor and World War II" would become "Students will be able to give three reasons why the Pearl Harbor attacks resulted in the United States engaging in war."

- ✏ "Students will be able to explain iambic pentameter" becomes "Students will be able to recognize and identify verses written in iambic pentameter; they will be able to define iambic pentameter, specifying the number of lines, rhythm pattern, and syllable count; finally, students will be able to construct their own poem in iambic pentameter."

✏ "Students know how to use the Pythagorean theorem" becomes "Students can use the Pythagorean theorem to calculate the length of one side of a triangle when given the other two."

You get the idea. Bottom line is, **if you think about how you can measure what you're trying to teach, you will write clearer objectives.** Then you are also able to pinpoint more accurately what you want students to know and to do by the end of that day's lesson. Moreover, you will write higher-level objectives. Clear objectives force you to parse out the basic recall (at the bottom of Bloom's taxonomy) from higher-level skills like comparing and contrasting, applying new information, supporting assertions with evidence, working cooperatively, judging the validity of sources and assertions, and communicating clearly. These more advanced skills are the ones we hope students take with them, but they require a higher level of mastery and warrant a higher grade, so it is helpful to distinguish them clearly.

Best of all, good objectives make you think about the assessment possibilities for the learner. By creating objectives that are measurable, **you have automatically devised the means by which you can assess** your students' skills and mastery of the content.

Require **A**ctive Participation

Now that you know exactly what you want students to be able to, how will you get them there? What activities will help them achieve those objectives? How will you get them engaged and excited about the material? And how will you know if they're successful?

These are the questions you ask as you look for the actual activities you will use to help students achieve the objectives. You want students to be actively engaged in the material, so you search out and steal a great hook or anticipatory set and activities that will keep students interested and active. Once you've found them, you add even more active participation by sprinkling in lots of opportunities to practice and process what they are learning through formal and informal assessments along the way.

Anticipatory Set

The "hook," or what most lesson models call "the anticipatory set," is **your attempt to engage students in the content to come** and get them thinking about the subject. Ideally, your hook is active, draws on students' prior knowledge, and relates to the day's objectives. Practically speaking, though, a great hook not only focuses students' attention on class, but also provides a great warm-up activity to get them engaged and give you time to take roll and other logistics.

While an anticipatory set can be a warm-up, a warm-up is not always an anticipatory set. So while I try to make my anticipatory set serve also as a warm-up, I have to remind myself that having a warm-up does not mean I have truly engaged the students in the content. I always have a warm-up, but sometimes it will not serve as an anticipatory set, which means I haven't yet really engaged students in the day's objectives. Whatever you may call it and however you may execute it, **find a way to make the upcoming content something relevant to the kids**.

The options for hooks are endless, of course, but it is still not easy to find something appropriate for every lesson. I want something that isn't so hard they're stumped, not so easy they finish too quickly, not so involved it takes too long, and not so predictable or typical that it bores them. So, like everything else we do, it's not easy! My tips? **Keep it interesting, keep it short, and keep it relevant**. Anything that gets the kids thinking is a great hook, so here are some examples that could be applied to any lesson.

Guess the topic. Students must guess the mystery concept or topic from the growing list I give them, which tells (misleadingly or cryptically at first) about that subject. An example for social science might be "Airplanes. Navy ships. Explosions. Hawaii. December 7, 1941" for Pearl Harbor. A science example could be "I am fast, not slow. I can leave or stay. I am outside, not in. I am negative, not positive. I am a particle, not an element" for electron.

Find the mistake. I give students one or more visuals, sample problems, written passages, quotes, worksheets, tables, figures, maps, charts, sample test questions, or other items that have a mistake. Their job is to determine what's wrong.

Explain the visual. Here students are treated to a short video, demonstration, discrepant event (puzzling or surprising phenomenon), model, or other visual and must explain what is happening.

Create a concept. Here I give students a collection of terms and have them create a visual, poem, song, concept map, KWL chart, brainstorming list, cartoon, chart, or other form of communication that puts it all together.

Take or make a quiz. Just as described, I simply write a few questions (or one good open-ended one) based on the week's objectives, and students must do their best to answer it correctly. Or, better still, I ask students to work alone or with a partner to create their own test or quiz question, suggesting they draw on the homework, a recent paper or project, a reading assignment, and so on.

This list is, of course, just a beginning. I am always adding ideas to my planning binder and stealing great hooks from outside resources, but this list of five gives me a jumping-off point and gives me a nice reminder of some of the directions in which I could go when I start to lose steam. While my science curriculum lends itself to doing a demonstration every day (and that would be lovely), it's just not feasible; but often I realize I can at least pass around an object or get a visual from the Internet that can get my students thinking.

I have to remind myself that **the anticipatory set doesn't have to be a huge undertaking (and shouldn't be)**. I keep answers short, but I stay committed to it because it gives me the administrative time I need, provides an additional assessment opportunity, and—most importantly—it gets students thinking. I find that making students commit their answers to writing is helpful in making them truly formulate an answer, so I employ a journal format in which each student responds to the anticipatory set and takes notes every day.

What I notice most about an anticipatory set (and closure) is that when I make the effort, I invariably reap the rewards. If I can capture their interest, the management problems, lethargy, and poor attitudes that can sometimes creep into any classroom are much less likely to do so. Better yet, I may actually get the students excited about the subject matter!

So the **advantages to using an anticipatory set** are many. It sets the tone for the class (all about learning), sets the tone for the students (time to work now), gets them thinking about the subject matter (science is cool!), gives you some information on what they've learned (so that's what's confusing them), *and* gives you a quiet, focused way to start class (priceless).

In terms of logistics, I save my **daily hooks in a PowerPoint presentation, followed by the day's objectives**, so I can present both easily to my students and have it all in digital format so I can use it year after year, edit as I go, and make notes for future reference. The students write their answers in a journal notebook that I can grade daily, weekly, or monthly as I choose.

Activities

You're about five minutes in. You've greeted your students, taken roll, engaged them in the topic of the day with your cool hook, and posted (and maybe even discussed) the day's objectives. Now what?

Your good, measurable objectives actually mean you've done most of the work already. You know what you want students to be able to do, so you just need to find activities that allow them to do it. **Remember that you are not the focus here—the students are.** What activities will help them learn the information that you already know so well? This is where that binder of possible activities that you've stolen from colleagues, found on the Internet, and borrowed or bought from other teachers comes into play. Don't reinvent the wheel! You *could* come up with your own original lesson, and sometimes it's worth it, but don't exhaust yourself doing that on a regular basis. Be a good thief; simply steal and adapt.

- ✏ Find activities you think will be engaging and that ask students to do the very things your objectives require of them. Use your curricular materials, your colleagues, and the web, and trust that your teaching can make an imperfect activity effective. **Try not to spend more time looking for a new activity than the time it will take to conduct it.** Of course, your planning will become more efficient with years of experience, but when you are out of time, trust that something you found will be good enough, and go with it.

☞ Vary the style and format of your lessons. Don't get stuck in a rut and use solely direct instruction (lecture, video, speaker), cooperative work (structured activities in which students must work together to complete a task), individual work (worksheets, reading, individual projects and papers), or group projects. Variety will keep the students engaged and will keep expanding your repertoire. **Try any new teaching model <u>at least</u> three times before making a final call on whether it works for you.**

☞ Whatever method of instruction you choose, **always follow the five-and-one rule** and incorporate lots of active participation (see below).

☞ Take copious notes. As you build your arsenal of activities, you'll have more and more great ideas from which to choose in the future, and you'll become a better and better judge about what works and what doesn't.

A note on direct instruction. I was a product of progressive instructors and was trained to scoff at direct instruction. What I've learned in the field is that there are always going to be particular topics or particular students for which/whom giving explicit, step-by-step instruction is the best way to communicate the information. So even if you're a die-hard constructivist, don't dismiss direct instruction completely. One simply needs to make direct instruction more interactive. Of course you'll try to make the information as engaging as possible, but besides whizbang visuals and great story-telling capabilities, the most effective way is through **active participation.** *As we all know from the failed empty-vessel analogy, you can't just stand up, spout information, and assume it will sink in.* **Students need repeated opportunities to process new information.** *That means lots of active participation.*

Active Participation

Keep students engaged by keeping them involved. You know their minds will wander. You know the blanket query "Any questions?" rarely produces some from those who have the most. So you have to use **checks for understanding** (otherwise known as formative assessments) frequently and creatively. My general list of go-to strategies follows, and there are plenty more on the web and in your neighboring classrooms. The crucial point is that the **checks must require active participation on the part of each individual student** and must occur frequently during the instruction. I've heard of folks following the ten-and-two rule (for every ten minutes of instruction, take two minutes to process or discuss it). **I prefer the five-and-one rule**. Every five minutes, take a one-minute break and ask students to think about and process each new piece of information. Here are my favorite strategies:

- Ask your neighbor a question about the material.
- Tell your neighbor something new you just learned.
- Tell your neighbor something you still don't understand.
- Recap or explain to a partner what we were just talking about.
- Answer my question and discuss or check the answer with a neighbor.
- Define a term to a neighbor and discuss if it's correct.
- Write down the answer to a question about the material just discussed.
- Write or orally define a term just given.
- Try an example or practice problem.
- Give a thumbs up/down or green-for-go/red-for-stop indication as to your level of understanding on the topic.
- Rate your understanding on a scale from one to ten.
- Draw a picture or graphic organizer representing the new information.
- Create a poem or haiku summing up the information.
- Write a slogan for a particular process or person.
- Create an acronym to remember a list of information.

Any way you can get students to stop and think about what they're learning so they internalize it and listen actively rather than passively is a winner, even if they do so alone. But getting them to discuss with a classmate is even better, since there's a greater level of investment and accountability.

Assessments

Ostensibly "assessment" is the last piece of any lesson, but as you've seen from the active participation strategies discussed above, **assessment shows up in *every* part of the lesson.** That's why I include it right in the meat of my lesson format with my "A" for active participation through the anticipatory set, activities, and assessments. I need to think about how I will assess my students every step of the way, as well as how I'll measure their learning at the end. **Assessment, therefore, should be thought of as the blanket step that is integrated into every other.**

The good news is that what you need to assess is directly specified in each of your objectives, and it can include any process by which you gather information from students about how well they are learning and understanding course content. You can gather this information in an informal manner (questions posed to students, homework and problem checks, and so on) or through more formal methods, such as tests and quizzes or written submissions. The main question is, are your students getting it? In other words, are you teaching effectively? As crucial as the answers to these questions seem, assessment is still commonly used as the final piece of a lesson and not **as feedback** to adjust our instructional methods, help our students, and inform our future teaching.

So as a check for myself, I make sure I am following the five-and-one rule during instruction and that I **have at least three forms of formative assessment and two forms of cumulative assessment** tied to every lesson.

Formative assessments: Active participation and checks for understanding during class, closure at the end of each class, homework

Cumulative assessments: Quizzes, tests, final unit test, unit projects

The **checks for understanding and active participation** are taken care of if I plan my lessons well. I make sure students are given multiple opportunities to process their learning each period, and I make sure at least one of those opportunities also gives me feedback on how each of them is doing (thumbs up or down, exit slip where students must answer a question before dismissal, and so on). Then closure, homework, quizzes, and projects provide even more opportunities for students to demonstrate their learning.

Process, Check, and Check Again

The rule of advertising is to (1) tell them what you're going to tell them, (2) tell them, and (3) tell them what you told them. This model is apt in the classroom as well. It is often hard to remember that students need at least seven exposures to something to become comfortable with it and twenty-one for it to become a habit. So another key element in planning your instruction is providing students with multiple opportunities for practice.

Guided Practice

Students' first opportunity to practice what they've learned is during the lesson, probably during one of your active participation/processing breaks. But most lessons will also include a practice time within the lesson, more formally known as "guided practice," which allows students to try out a newly learned skill on their own, but with assistance available, if necessary. This tends to be the meat of my class period—**the chance for students to be let loose with the material.**

You have already worked lots of guided practice in through all your active participation. But to get in those twenty-one repetitions that will help students master the objective, you want an activity where students are required to practice the new skill you've taught them—ideally an authentic activity that will interest your students and where they can really get their hands dirty and explore the topic with their peers.

If you've been feeling restricted by the traditional lesson plan format, wishing you could use more constructivist methods, this is your chance. Here's where you can have a great constructivist activity, project-based learning, cooperative activity, or collaborative project to get students really immersed in the material. In science you might conduct a lab or create a model; in math you might use manipulatives or creative problem solving; in language arts you might edit a piece of writing piece of writing, write a blog entry, or complete a brochure or letter exchange or diary; in social sciences you might create a slide presentation or a skit or timeline or analyze a historical document. Or you might have students practice their new skills in simpler, short term methods, but whatever you do, they are practicing and mastering the new information.

Processing and Closure

One more opportunity students will have to practice (or process) the material is during the conclusion of your lesson. Lesson formats call this "closure," and it is probably the most missed and poorly executed element of any lesson. Standing at the front of the class and summing up what was covered is *not* closure. Just like your checks for understanding, **closure requires the active participation of each student**. What you want is another active participation strategy like a thumbs up/thumbs down, thought question, practice problem, or simple recall question. You can do this in a pair-share format, game-show format, exit-slip format, or whatever method you like. You just want to make sure you've had the opportunity to get all your students to see for themselves (and subsequently for you) whether they've achieved that day's objective.

I also think **consistent closure is indicative of effective teaching**. If you're doing a great job including processing opportunities all lesson long, closure doesn't need to be cumbersome, but it does indicate a level of professionalism and a commitment to keeping your students engaged and focused right up until the end.

Independent Practice

Usually just a fancy name for homework, independent practice *can* be completed after class when the students are on their own, but **it should not be relegated to work done outside school hours**. Students should practice independently in school as well, so you can see what they are capable of doing on their own. It's important to give students the opportunity to apply their new content or skills without assistance. It also helps to stress to students that you want them practicing *independently*, because assigning something for homework certainly doesn't guarantee that they'll complete the task alone or fully master it.

The importance of independent practice also means **you don't assign homework for its own sake, but only when independent practice is truly warranted**. For example, when students try to understand the structure of the atom, independent reading and exploration are a good start, but will do only so much. My ability to explain, show visuals, and use analogies is often most helpful to students. However, when students are trying to master writing chemical formulas, I can explain the concept for them, but only practice will truly teach them how to do so reliably.

So homework needs to serve the proper purpose. As one stolen and rather irreverent saying goes, **homework should be like a miniskirt: long enough to cover the important stuff and short enough to keep it interesting**. Bottom line, we need to assign work that is truly relevant, manageable, and meaningful for the student, both in the amount of time it will take and in its difficulty. If students do practice independently in class and demonstrate mastery, additional independent practice (or homework) isn't always necessary.

I try to stress to students that there are really **two types of homework**. In some cases (as in a "flipped" classroom model where I ask students to read the text or watch a video), I am asking students to take in **new information**, assimilate it the best they can, and come to class to have it clarified. The second type of homework is **practice**. While many students see homework as mundane busy work, I emphasize that it is really their opportunity to gain mastery and automaticity, and see if they can do the work *on their own*, without help, like they would on a test. That may involve simple practice of what they did in class, or it may involve taking what they learned in class and applying it to new situations, just as they might on a test.

So my goals for homework are that students get a chance to do the following:

- ✏ practice what they've learned
- ✏ learn new information, noting what is confusing
- ✏ try out what they've learned in new situations

They don't necessarily need a lot of homework to do these things. In fact, as you'll see in the Grading chapter, students can still earn an A in my class without doing any homework. Nonetheless, I assign it when I think it will help the students, and I try to be reasonable without sacrificing high expectations. When assigning homework, I keep in mind the reasons I give it: to read and explore new content, to practice using it, and to help students master a skill. For more demanding courses, it is also to learn new information and be prepared to discuss or build on in it during the next class. So I make it short, relevant, and useful, and I try to keep it interesting.

Some **ways to manage the homework load**: Instead of assigning twenty practice problems, I may let them choose two from each section. I might have them create their own questions to bring in about the material. Students can be required to prepare a visual summary, or create their own homework assignment. I use activators/guiding schema (concept maps, outlines, and other types of scaffolding) to help students approach new information. For example, unless you are teaching students how to take notes from a text (not a bad idea, by the way, since few students ever formally learn this), a better homework assignment than "Read and take notes on chapter 4" would be "Read these anticipatory questions, then read chapter 4, then go back and answer the questions given," or "Read chapter 4 and complete

How much homework is too much homework?

Homework has been getting a bad rap lately, with the amount of homework steadily increasing and parents and students alike becoming more and more exasperated by the workload. This is why having a solid philosophy of homework is so important. You want to be able to justify your assignments to students and parents alike when they ask why you assign what you do. Be open to feedback, but make sure not to be blind to the person giving it. You will get a feel for the students who are earnestly trying in class, and these conscientious, struggling students are your most valuable voice in this regard. Your top students will often think the workload is fine because they are able to complete it so easily and quickly. The unmotivated students will think any amount is too much. But the hard workers, especially those who are struggling with the material are the ones to whom you'll want to listen most closely. Not only is their feedback likely to be honest and fair, but you don't want to alienate or crush these students with too much work and risk pushing them to the point of giving up.

the concept map I've started for you." Your better students may not need this type of guidance, but they will hardly suffer from it, while your weaker students will benefit.

JOB 4: KEEP IT REAL

At this point, you are surely convinced that your lesson planning will take hours and that the lesson itself has so many important elements that you can't possibly fit them all in, especially in a traditional fifty-minute period. To that I say, you are correct! So keep a few additional points in mind as you plan lesson after lesson.

Stick to a Schedule

Set yourself a scheduled time for planning, and stick to it. I know veteran teachers who still put in twelve-hour days. I commend them, but I don't want to be them. I want to be so good I can achieve those results in an eight- or nine-hour day. I want a life. So schedule your planning time, and when it's up, trust in what you have and move on to the next thing.

Within reason, you want to do the same during class, and this is one problem I do have with lesson plans. While all the important aspects of the teaching are addressed, that format is often little help in planning the logistics of the actual class. While the objectives get most of the ink and time in my planning, the learning activities get the majority of the time in the classroom. There's a disconnect, then, between the planning emphasis and the execution emphasis, but when I abandoned my lesson-planning template in favor of a grocery list of tasks during class, I found that my focus and execution of them suffered.

My lessons are almost always going to have some amount of direct instruction and guided practice, but it's easy to leave out the anticipatory set, clear objectives, and closure. When I make the effort to include each of those elements, my lessons (and student response and learning) are better as a result. I still need to have the road map in my head, even if it isn't anything that's particularly evident to students. So I have a cheat sheet that lists each of the key lesson plan elements, but also has space for an **agenda** which is the real time plan of execution:

- ✏ taking roll/anticipatory set (five minutes)
- ✏ record/review homework (five minutes)
- ✏ explain today's activity (five minutes)

- ✏ cooperative activity (twenty minutes)
- ✏ sharing out (ten minutes)
- ✏ clean-up (five minutes)
- ✏ closure (five minutes)

This simplified agenda doesn't show all the active participation strategies and assessements, but it's in there because of the advanced planning I did on the rest of the page. During class, however, this is the road map that I really use to keep myself on schedule.

Go with the Flow

Once you've planned that perfect lesson, it can be hard to let go, but you do need to **be willing to revise and adapt as you go**. This lesson format is certainly not the be-all, end-all to lesson planning, and **by no means should any lesson model be seen as inviolate or constrictive**. For example, while this lesson format is intended for a single lesson conducted in a single sitting, it is likely that a given lesson can be better conducted in pieces over many classes. I have found that in my efforts to make sure each element is present, my lessons can become a bit long and too regimented and won't provide for the odd tangent that may lead to a great teachable moment. The format is also for relatively small, discrete lessons and doesn't lend itself as well to long-term assignments. But it is a great place to start.

While many lesson formats may work as well or better for general lesson planning, this three-part-lesson format is a nice summary of elements—most of which, it just so happens, *will* be part of any comprehensive lesson plan. It is also general enough that you can incorporate into it many other teaching methods (cooperative learning, group projects, and so on) to fit your own style.

But no matter what style you choose, the key is remembering to **check that each lesson has a measurable objective, lots of active participation and assessments, and plenty of opportunities for practice.** If you analyze your lessons, you will hopefully find that each of these elements is there, each serving its own important purpose, but you can never go wrong laying them all out clearly beforehand.

The lesson plan isn't the only thing that matters, but by tying myself to a lesson plan, the most critical elements are more often included and the opportunities for students to internalize and review their learning are more frequent and more effective. Best of all, by having a solid framework to which I generally stick, I have the freedom (with less fallout) to stray once in a while.

4

GRADING SMART

JOB 1:   **KNOW WHAT THE GRADE REPRESENTS**
- Set Your Standard
- Communicate with Rubrics

JOB 2:   **DECIDE WHAT GOES INTO THE GRADE**
- Determine Course Requirements
- Weigh Them Appropriately

JOB 3:   **SET UP YOUR SYSTEM**
- Break It Down and Assign Worth
- Extra Credit? Try Contract Projects

JOB 4:   **SOK IT TO 'EM**
- Grade <u>S</u>mart
- Grade <u>O</u>ften
- Grade <u>K</u>indly

JOB 5:   **ANTICIPATE OBJECTIONS**
- Why that Grade?
- Accommodations
- The Big Picture

JOB 6:   **GO HOME HAPPY**
- "They Go Home Tired. You Go Home."
- Expect the Best

The aspect of teaching that tends to be most constant, most contentious, and most cumbersome is grading. If there is an element of the job that burns teachers out the quickest, this is it. Not only is it difficult to give so many students sincere, valuable feedback on each and every assignment, it gets especially discouraging when students don't always read and use that feedback. So this chapter focuses on helping you find smart, efficient methods for grading that provide effective feedback for you and your students without taking up all your free time.

JOB 1: KNOW WHAT THE GRADE REPRESENTS

First, you must be grounded in what you want a student's grade to represent, so you know what to grade, how carefully, how frequently, and for what weight. Think about the options. Are you going to grade on effort or accuracy? Will you grade each assignment, a sampling, or will you look at growth over time? Will you assign points or a letter grade? How much will each assignment be worth in comparison to others? How will you ensure that your final grade communicates what it should about that student's performance?

Set Your Standards

Let's start with the big picture. What should a grade really mean? **Check with colleagues and set your standard.** I believe a student's grade should represent the level to which they've mastered the standards. An A should indicate mastery of the subject matter or standards taught in your class. A B should indicate a solid working knowledge. A C should indicate a basic level of understanding. A D should suggest only superficial understanding or a lack of understanding of core principles, and an F indicates failure to master most or all of the standards.

Communicate It with Rubrics

See my sample rubric with a description of A-level writing below, and check out plenty of others online (sites like rubrics4teachers.com and teach-nology.com are great resources). **Rubrics written in clear, descriptive language are a useful way to define for you as well as for students and parents exactly what type of work each letter grade represents.** Use them, but be sure you "own" what they say. What I like most about detailed rubrics is that I can circle the items represented in a given paper and the preponderance of marks then shows the grade category most closely represented by that student's work.

The overall grade for the class follows the same principle. You should have an idea what each grade really means, and it should be one that your colleagues and administration could support.

Bloom's taxonomy is another useful tool as you plan your grading criteria. An A ideally won't be earned simply by memorizing sufficient facts to pass knowledge-recall tests. An A should represent a level of mastery that allows the student to engage in higher levels of critical thinking: applying the knowledge to new situations, solving problems using creative solutions, and evaluating others' solutions.

Sample Rubric

Here is an excerpt from a position paper rubric,
showing the distinct levels of achievement in each grading area.

	Thesis	*Organization*
A = Exemplary	Takes a strong, well-defined position; uses at least four appropriate reasons with at least three supporting details for each reason	Writer demonstrates logical sequencing of ideas through well-developed paragraphs; transitions are used to enhance organization; a gripping introduction and a strong conclusion.
B = Admirable	Clear position taken and defined; some reasons and some details present but not fully developed	Paragraph development present but sometimes illogical sequencing; introduction and conclusion included.
C = Acceptable	Position not clearly stated; development is brief; unrelated, unsupported general statements, reasons, and details; minimal facts used	Paragraph development present but not perfected; introduction and/or conclusion absent.
D = Attempted	No clear position taken; undeveloped reasons; no facts used	No evidence of thoughtful paragraph structure; no introduction or conclusion; illogical organization of ideas

In other words, A work should be of such nature that it could be put on reserve for all students to review and emulate. The A student is, in fact, an example for others to follow. B work indicates high quality performance and is given recognition for solid work; a B should be considered a high grade. C work represents average/satisfactory work. A student receiving a C has met the requirements, including deadlines, of the course.

JOB 2: DECIDE WHAT GOES INTO THE GRADE

Determine Course Requirements

You know what you want your grade to communicate. Now think about what tasks best represent that level of mastery. For a literature course, the importance of written assignments may justify placing greater weight on those and lesser weight on tests, and likely the opposite for math. For a language course, oral exams may be important; for the social sciences, projects. For science and other hands-on classes, labs, or performance assessments may be the most important components.

Weigh Them Appropriately

You can certainly just dive in and assign points as you go, but I think it preferable to **list the components you think will make up your course grade and decide how much each piece should matter in the grade as a whole.** Should the grade be based mostly on test scores or classwork or homework? What is an appropriate balance, and how should it be calculated? Is it simply an average of points earned over the course of a semester, or do you give holistic grades based on performance and overall achievement? How do you ensure your grades are not subjective? How do you make sure other teachers' grades mean the same thing yours do and communicate the proper level of learning to other educational institutions? How do you motivate students with grades without minimizing the value of the learning? Should you offer extra credit? How often should you grade students and in what ways? And how do you do so effectively without mountains of work?

The answers all depend on your own philosophy and that of your department and school, and on your subject area. For science, my grade split tends to be 10 percent on homework, 30 percent on labs, and 60 percent on tests. For an elective video course I taught, the breakdown was 20 percent homework, 20 percent tests, and 60 percent video projects. For beginning algebra, it was 40 percent homework, 10 percent projects, 50 percent tests. Because I believe **the grade should represent what that student can do on his or her own with that subject matter**, tests (or similar performance assessments) tend to warrant a large portion of the grade. But for a video course, where the essential skills are being able to work as part of a team, performing various production roles, and creating a film, the project grade (earned as part of a team) is the most crucial.

For younger students or for classes where homework-completion habits are critical, I make homework count for a significant part of the grade. For older, more responsible students, I know that some can do little to no homework and still master the material. I don't think those students should be penalized, so in those courses homework counts for 10 percent. That means they can still earn an A- or 90 percent with a zero in homework.

Talk to your colleagues. Find out what projects they use and how they calculate their grades. If your grading system is imposed on you by the district or department, ask as many questions as necessary so you are comfortable with it and can defend it. Once you have a good idea what level of mastery and performance those assignments should warrant, you can more easily make decisions about how your day-to-day grading should work.

JOB 3: SET UP YOUR SYSTEM

Break It Down and Assign Worth

Let's use this sample breakdown:
- homework, 10 percent
- projects, 30 percent
- tests, 60 percent

You could assign points for every assignment so your totals worked out this way at the end, but it is far easier to **use grading software**, which makes the weighted grades easier to calculate and easier to communicate to students and parents as each grade is immediately calculated and averaged separately.

I use a point system, assigning what I feel are appropriate point values to each assignment within its area (homework, projects, tests), and then I let my grading software total and average those points to give an overall grade for each section. It weighs each section the appropriate amount and combines those totals to make the overall course grade. That way, **when any of us look at the grade, we can see a homework average, a project average, and a test average, and see immediately where a given student is struggling or excelling.** I check each grade at progress report dates and semester's end to ensure they are a fair representation for each student, and my goal is always to ensure the grade truly represents each student's mastery of the material.

Homework: 10 Percent

Homework could easily be worth *nothing.* It is a chance for students to practice and master the material, and I am comfortable with the idea that if students get it the first time, they shouldn't need to continue that practice unless speed is also one of the components of mastery. Moreover, homework is essentially represented in students' papers, projects, and tests, because those students who have done the practice to achieve mastery will do better on those assessments.

However, I recognize that it is demoralizing for students to complete homework night after night for no evident payoff. More importantly, not grading or counting homework provides no motivation and gives students permission *not* to do the necessary work in order to achieve mastery. From this perspective, homework should be worth much *more* than 10 percent, but the volume of daily homework often means you will elect to check more for effort than accuracy.

It is also true that for some students homework will not translate into mastery, so making homework worth more would not be a fair measure of their skills. 10 percent works for me because **it makes or breaks one letter grade**. The students who can ace everything just by reading it once can skip homework completely and still earn an A-, and solid effort on homework by students who really struggle can get them one letter grade higher than their test scores.

Projects: 30 Percent

Making up about a third of my grade are long-term projects. Since many are completed as part of a team, these projects do not always reflect a student's individual effort, so I do not feel comfortable making these worth a larger percentage of the grade, but I do like that a significant portion does depend on a student's ability to work cooperatively. I assign the papers, projects, and lab reports relative point values that seem appropriate within the projects category and then average those for a general project grade.

Tests: 60 Percent

This category gets the heaviest weight. *If* I am using good tests, graded fairly, tests should represent most clearly how much my students have mastered the material because they are truly individual efforts. Therefore, tests represent the largest portion of the grade. You've heard the saying, "Don't teach to the test," but **we should have no problem teaching to the test if it's a good test!** The challenge, then, is to design tests that are a fair measure of students' knowledge and that are graded in a way that properly reflects that. See the subsequent section for more on that.

One can defend any number of percentage breakdowns; do what feels right to you. But this system provides a clear grading structure that helps me pinpoint where students are struggling and also helps me communicate student grades clearly and easily. **The percentages can also be motivating**: students who do their homework religiously but struggle with tests can still be proud of earning an A in homework; students who don't do their homework or who don't put much effort into their writing can see right away how that impacts their grade in other areas.

It's always a good idea to warn students and parents, especially with an online grading system, that the grades may seem odd the first few weeks when there are only a few assignments entered in each area. After the first two weeks of class, ten homework assignments nicely average for a homework total, but one lab is counting for 30 percent of the grade and two quizzes the other 60 percent. This can result in some startling grade totals. Assure them it will provide a more balanced reflection as the semester progresses.

Extra Credit? Try Contract Projects

Since I believe the grade should represent what students know about the subject and not how helpful or well-behaved they were, **I am not a fan of bonus points and extra credit.** I do think students should be afforded **opportunities to improve** their grades, but I believe they should earn that improved grade in ways that reflect a deeper understanding of the content, such as revising a paper or project, or retaking a test.

Contract Projects

There is **one important opportunity I give students to improve their grade that I call "contract projects."** I make a variety of outside learning activities available to students, and they can choose, or contract out, their own grade. To earn an

A, the student must complete a sufficient number of assignments. Each assignment is worth ten to thirty points, as I deem appropriate, and I offer students the opportunity to earn up to 100 points, so they decide which grade they earn by how many projects they complete. As a bonus, I count this as a test grade, so it is a key opportunity for students to improve their test average.

Examples include reading relevant books or articles related to the course and reporting on them, researching and answering a "stump the teacher" question (addressing a question I couldn't answer in class), or attending Homework Club (after-school tutorial) and assisting other students. I add to the list as I see fit. The possibilities are endless, and sometimes students come up with their own ideas, like a trip to a science museum. As long as the idea is academically focused, I let the student know I don't accept extra credit, but their proposed activity could count as a contract project.

My favorite contract project is having students come in after school to help other students; that way they learn the material better and earn points as well. Obviously, the student has to be clear enough on the content, but if she can do that, it's a win-win for everyone.

There are lots of things I like about contract projects: the flexibility and catchall nature of the work students can complete, the opportunity to extend learning outside the classroom, and the fact that I am giving students the chance to earn whatever grade they are willing to work for. In addition, **contract projects provide a wonderful management tool**. Students should never be sitting idle in class, because if they are done with the day's work, they can still be working on a contract project.

JOB 4: SOK IT TO 'EM

Effective grading has long been my albatross. If it weren't for the time spent grading, I might actually get home by five with*out* a huge pile of work. Grading can make or break you as a teacher. These are the piles of work that wait for you after school, and this is the work that feels most thankless. It is repetitive and time consuming—and worse, we can pour our hearts into it only to find our students tossing it aside. That's why efficient and effective grading strategies are so important.

I came into the teaching profession with the **old-fashioned view of grading**: that it would be the final judgment, the last word after a series of practice runs. But as my lesson road-MAP hammers home, that assessment **needs to come early and often** and be focused less on a grade and more on the feedback for learning. I work hard to remind myself and my students that their assignments are opportunities for learning and are *not* intended to be summative demonstrations of their knowledge. The grade is not as important as the feedback; students need to use these assignments as learning experiences, and we need to tailor our grading accordingly.

To help myself stick to the program, I've devised these principles: I "SOK" it to grading by **grading Smart, grading Often, and grading Kindly.** Grading smart means using strategies that keep my workload manageable and minimize the impact on my time and (let's face it) patience, while still maximizing the efficacy of the feedback students get on their work. I am always looking to steal ideas that help me to grade more effectively and efficiently. Next I try to grade often, since this is a key factor in proactively managing student learning rather than playing catch-up or worse, back-up. Finally, when I say I grade kindly, I don't mean I go easy on students, but I do make the effort to "accentuate the positive" about every student effort.

Grade Smart

How do you give each student's work the attention it deserves without working yourself silly? First, **choose wisely what must be graded in the first place**. One of the reasons I got buried in grading my first few years was my compulsion to collect and examine every piece of work my students completed. Stemming from my innate need for control, this tendency should not have been surprising, and while laudable, it is not necessarily more effective. As you ponder a pile of papers, consider whether it will be more helpful for your students if you spend that hour writing comments on their work (which they may or may not read), on planning a better lesson, or on some well-deserved down time so you'll be fresh in the morning. For many assignments, it can be just as effective to give students a completion grade (simply checking off that they did the work and giving credit/points based on completion rather than mastery) or have students check their own work in class. Here are some smart grading strategies:

- ✐ Pick two to three examples and grade only those
- ✐ Have students circle the problems they found most challenging and give feedback on those.
- ✐ Give students a quiz from the homework, and grade just that.
- ✐ Pick two to three examples and have students grade them in pair-shares or as a class.

- Display the key, and have students grade their own work or that of a neighbor and discuss common areas of difficulty in pairs, groups, or as a class.
- Have students pick a problem with which they struggled and share/solve only those in class.
- Have students compare answers in groups and share those on which they didn't agree.

I make it a point to **put the onus on the students** to find their mistakes and judge their learning whenever possible. This is new for many students, so there will be a learning curve. You will need to double-check their grading at first, but as you learn who is reliable, you will soon learn which submissions will require more careful analysis. Then, as students become more comfortable finding their own mistakes, they will become more skilled at doing so before the grading process, and you will have students who are more self-sufficient.

Here are some examples of ways to help shift the grading responsibility to the student:

- Have students complete quiz or test corrections for homework.
- Rather than giving students a quiz with two problems marked wrong and the correct answers written in, return the quiz with a note at the top that two of the problems are wrong and that their homework for that night is to find which two and correct them.
- Give students a checklist or rubric, and have them turn in their assignment when they can justify it has met all the criteria.

- ✏ Have students provide feedback on a partner's work before submission (with explicit guidance on how to do so, such as providing three positives and two improvements that they can tie directly to the assignment guidelines or rubric).

- ✏ Have students keep their work in a portfolio that will be graded intermittently on its evidence of learning, self-assessment, and growth.

These strategies not only help you use your time more effectively, but also make students take responsibility for the accuracy of their work and for thinking more deeply about their learning.

One more strategy that will help your grading is something you are already doing: choosing your assignments carefully. Extend that smart planning to include consideration of how you will grade each assignment, and if any particular job still looks daunting, **pare down the grading by focusing on one or two key concepts on the assignment.** You may get the objection from students that they didn't know you would grade wholly on those two areas, so let them know ahead of time or treat it as a learning experience. Students should complete the entire assignment thoroughly, since you chose it as a great opportunity for practice or further learning for them, and they should always come in for help before it's due if they are struggling with any area, but especially because you may grade only one or two key areas.

You can effectively grade many assignments **on effort alone** with a simple check confirming it was completed, because **if students fake it, they are only cheating themselves.** (Or, as I often tell them, "You may be able to snow me, but you can't snow

---

Grading Smart

Don't collect everything, and don't grade every piece of what you collect. You'll get the most bang for your buck if you do the following:

- Empower students by showing them how to assess their own work.
- Teach students how to give each other feedback.
- Emphasize effort and progress through completion grades and portfolios.
- Focus on the key concepts and areas for improvement on any assignment.
- Use the tools at your disposal: student aides, electronic scoring, and so on.

God.") Their lack of effort will certainly show up later on quizzes or tests, and a poor completion grade is still giving students the crucial feedback that they may be at risk.

Don't forget to make use of other tools that may be at your disposal. Delegating work to parent volunteers or teachers' aides may be acceptable for many assignments. Electronically graded answer sheets and other computer-based programs that help score students and provide feedback are also fabulous tools.

Finally, **learn from the experts**. Observe which teachers are teaching effectively but still leaving at a reasonable hour, and beg, borrow, and steal whatever strategies they are using.

As an overly thorough type-A personality, resisting the urge to check every problem and every word has been tough for me, but the extra moment I take to ask myself, "Is this really necessary?" is always worth it. I weigh the benefits of grading it myself, outside of class, against the drawbacks of taking time in class to do it. I generally prefer to save that class time for other activities, but sometimes I realize that going over a particular assignment will be a meaningful learning expe-rience. Most importantly, I remind myself that **the students should be putting more effort into their work than the teacher**. If they didn't give the assignment more than thirty seconds, I cer-tainly shouldn't. Instead, I ask for a redo after school when I can be there to help them.

> **Remember that the *student* should be putting more time and effort into their work than you are!**

I also remind myself that the students are getting lots of feed-back in other ways. All those active participation strategies, discus-sion during pair-shares, question and answer sessions, and group discussions are among the many types of feedback they receive in class each day, so when I approach the piles of papers or computer submissions waiting for me after my students have gone home for the day, I remind myself that I don't have to write a treatise on each of their assignments. I **give them the minimum feedback re-quired to help them improve.**

Grade Often

Why grade often? The more often you grade students, the more feedback you and they both get on their learning. More importantly, you help students catch their mistakes before they become habits, you root out prior misconceptions, and you keep students encouraged and affirmed. You're steering the rocket ship, constantly adjusting and correcting, helping students not fall behind or go astray.

I tell students that mistakes are not only expected but necessary, and goofing up on their work should be a point of pride, not embarrassment, since mistakes show they are trying something new, moving forward, and putting themselves out there enough that they might not get everything right every time. **Remind students that they actually help themselves by making more mistakes and catching them early.**

As you MAP your lesson, you are already planning your many assessments. First, the **anticipatory set** and **closure** will help you get a quick real-world look at where students are for each and every class. It's quick and easy because it's habit and you grade it then and there.

Second, the **active participation** in class provides the next level of feedback—the discussion questions, the thumbs up/thumbs downs, the pair-shares. Students are constantly thinking and providing information so that you have a continuous read on the "temperature" of the room. Are they engaged? Are they getting it? Are they able to take the next step? Are they ready for the next part of the lesson? You are not always the one providing that feedback to the student—their fellow students can serve that function as well—but you are getting feedback as you look around the room.

Third, as you use a large variety of small and frequent **assessments**, students are getting more frequent feedback and seeing how they are doing before the unit has passed them by.

Grade Kindly

This final rule of grading has been **the most important change to my grading since I began teaching**. After realizing my tough grading was sometimes a bit demoralizing for even my adult students, I adopted a new policy: provide at least two positive comments for each suggested improvement. I also worked to shift my focus and see myself as a cheerleader more than a correctional officer, reshaping the *wording* of my comments to be more positive as well.

While this shift felt a little disingenuous at first, as I forced myself to come up with a list of positives, even after reading an abysmal essay, I couldn't argue with the amazing improvement in the results. First, it forced me to soften that critical eye and really see the things they were already doing right. Second, students were much less discouraged by my comments and more willing to tackle the problems I saw. **I'd found a system that actually encouraged, rather than discouraged, future effort.**

In retrospect, the reason is obvious. (And you knew this all along, yes?) People like to hear what they are doing right. I made the mistake of assuming they would realize that all the stuff I

Accentuate the Positive

1. **Keep in mind the purpose of grading: helping students learn.**
2. **Keep it positive: two pluses for every drawback.**
3. **Cast problem areas as opportunities for improvement.**

Assignment Feedback

Before

Nice effort on this persuasive essay, but your thesis is not clearly stated and your support for it is rather weak. Remember, you want to give three good reasons supporting your assertion and then three details supporting each reason. These are lacking. Grade: 5/10. F

After

You have chosen a provocative subject that is engaging to the reader. I like that you think to use an anecdote to open the essay and catch our attention, and your writing is clear and straightforward. Here is what would make the essay even stronger: the issue is a sticky one so you need to state your thesis very clearly right away, then give at least three reasons supporting it, each with clear facts supporting those. These are lacking, and since this was the crux of the assignment, your score is 5/10. F

---

didn't mention must have been fine, so if I pointed out just the areas that needed improvement, they could surmise that the other areas were just great. But of course it's not that simple. If I don't mention it at all, does that mean it was just acceptable, terrific, or just not as bad as the parts I did mention? So, while at first my explicit affirmations seemed like transparent efforts to "butter up" my students, the truth was I was providing much-needed confirmation about their areas of success.

Of course, that doesn't mean you don't assign an F when it is warranted, but hopefully you **do so in a way that acknowledges the student's effort (or even just their potential, if the effort isn't there)**, and points out to the student what he or she needs to do to improve that grade. In this particular aspect, your grading may take a little bit longer, but it will be so much more happily received—and truly read! And if you are following the earlier advice of grading smart, you can spare the time to grade kindly.

One final point: as I often have to remind my students, **we don't give students their grades; they earn them.** You will often hear the question "Why did you give me a C

> **You don't *give* students grades; they *earn* them.**

on this paper?" As tedious as it becomes, I always start my reply with the correction "First of all, I didn't give you that grade, you earned it." Then I generally ask why *they* think it might have only warranted a C grade and why they think that was not an accurate assessment. Those discussions are usually quite enlightening.

JOB 5: ANTICIPATE OBJECTIONS

Since grading is such an important and personal aspect of teaching, it may be helpful to consider a few common challenges and suggested responses.

Why that Grade?

"Why don't you grade on a curve?" My response to students is, "Do you really think this will help you?" I generally take one day each year when I show what "grading on a curve" really means. Even if most students earn B work, a curve forces some into the A and some into the C range artificially. That might help some, but it also hurts some. Most of all, it is no longer a true representa-

tion of their learning if, criterion-wise, they learned a B's worth of material. This concern is most often voiced by students when they think everyone is doing poorly, so I assure them that if they all bomb a test, I will look closely at what occurred. If the test was too hard, too early, or did not fairly represent what I taught them, I adjust the scores or throw them out. If they simply didn't study, they get what they earned.

"Why did you give me a C on this project?" My go-to answer: "I don't assign grades; you earn them." I take every opportunity to point out to students that **I go to great lengths to lay out clear and thorough guidelines so that I don't have to decide what grades to give them.** I have a key, a well-crafted test or rubric, and I follow my guidelines to determine what amount of learning is shown and therefore what grade they have earned according to the standards set out. So I say, "You mean, why did you earn a C on that paper? Why don't you tell me?" I'm really not trying to drive them crazy or shut them down, but I think the semantics are worth noting. Once they take responsibility for the work, a sit-down showing them how to improve it is more productive.

"Can I do some extra credit?" Ah, extra credit—the quick-fix grade panacea. I love when my students come to me with the age-old question "Isn't there any extra credit I can do to bring up my grade?" Hmm, and what did you have in mind? Their answer is especially enlightening; it is usually something unrelated to class such as cleaning the white boards, helping to organize a storage room, or creating a poster. At least the last one could be adapted to something academic, but more often extra credit is not, and this is my main objection.

Even when we put aside the fact that extra credit is not fair to other students, it is also unjustified as part of the grade since it is often unrelated to the state standards or the content students are expected to master, and it sends the wrong message to those viewing their final grade. Instead, I direct students to contract projects: their one flexible way of improving their grade through creative and content-focused work. I also take the opportunity to **reiterate the importance of working harder on the assignments already given**. If I am sympathetic to the students' plight (meaning they are truly sincere and not just wanting to make a quick-fix, last-ditch effort), I may accept past assignments if they are greatly improved.

This could also be seen as unfair to other students, (more on this in the following section,) but I make clear that this is another example of communication being crucial to success in my class. If other students approached me and made the same plea, I'd likely make them the same offer. But this is the student before me today. I might give him work to make up, but it has to be justified and has to demonstrate improved mastery of the standards for it to affect his grade.

Accommodations

"Can I try again [redo the assignment]?" In general, when deciding whether to give students a second chance, I consider the following: How many chances have they had? Will doing this assignment again actually help them learn it? How can I give them another opportunity that is fair to them, fair to the other students, and fair to me? If I give this opportunity to one student, will others want and need the same consideration? I planned a course that already provides for second chances, so is this an earnest request from a student who has been diligent, or is it a last-ditch effort from a student who has been unmotivated until now?

Any appropriate accommodation at this stage of the game (for a student who has no special need requiring accommodation) should create new work for the student *without* creating a lot of new work for me. While our main focus as teachers is on students and their learning of content standards, some of the preparation students get in school is on life skills like time management, responsibility, and communication. In my experience, tough love is almost always more effective and better respected by students, parents, and administrators alike. So the question is, have they been taking advantage of each opportunity and simply need more chances to prove their learning, or have they let opportunities slip by? If the latter is the case, they are responsible for taking advantage of the opportunities given, and I am not responsible for making more.

"But I'm a terrible test taker!" We've all encountered the student who feels his performance in class does not truly represent his level of knowledge. I treat these on a case-by-case basis. If I have a student with test anxiety, I will do whatever necessary to make her more comfortable, but I also remind her that she will need to complete applications and tests for all sorts of things out in the "real world," and rarely are accommodations made for people there. You get the driver's test in the neighborhood around the DMV, and that's where you have to take it. The SATs are offered in a certain location and that's where you get to take them. So I make myself available to help students work through whatever problems they have, and if they show significant improvement, I'm willing to take that into account when calculating the final grade (see the following section). But ultimately they still need to be able to prove in a variety of ways that they've mastered the content.

The Big Picture

"How do you decide on final grades?" Most of the time, I don't. I work hard during the year to make sure my grades properly reflect student learning. If I've done that, the grade that presents itself to me at the end of a semester should be accurate. I do a few things to help me feel confident about that: (1) I enter actual letter grades in addition to numbers in my grade book. I like to be able to look through and see how students have been doing overall on labs, homework, and tests, without just seeing numbers. Are they generally getting A's, Bs, or Cs? If I can see that at a glance, it gives a fuller picture more quickly to me, the student, and their parents. (2) I keep each of their progress report grades handy throughout the year. Are they consistent? Is something drastically different this time? If so, was it a fluke? And (3) I check the percentage and where it sits in relation to the next cutoff.

I do *not* let the computer round up for me—I look at the strict percentage—but **this is my chance to exercise some professional discretion**. Did she earn 89.52 percent? If so, it is very likely I will bump her up to an A-, unless she eked out that 89.52 percent and a B+ is a fairer reflection of the amount of chemistry she knows. I think the grade can include some reflection of the student's work ethic, but in the end it is most important that it reflect her knowledge of the subject matter. Generally, whenever contemplating a grade boost, I consider the following: Did she complete all her assignments? As I mentioned with regard to second chances, **if it wasn't important enough to her to do the work to bring up the grade in the first place, why should I do it for her now?** Did she show improvement or at least consistency? If she began to slack off toward the end, she was again telling me the grade wasn't that important. What is her true knowledge of chemistry? If her labs showed solid understanding of the concepts of chemistry, and a low test grade at the start of the semester is what's pulling down her average, perhaps an A- really is the most appropriate grade.

But the flipside is a tricky one. What if she *did* slack off, did not turn in assignments, and generally did not care about the grade, but she is incredibly bright, aced all her tests, and met the standards of the course? This student may really know an A's-worth of chemistry, but because it's so easy for her, she didn't bother with the homework. Well, again, if the grade mattered to her, she could keep that A by tutoring others, doing enough homework to get by, and so on. So the grade likely stands, because her work habits and diligence should be reflected in the grade to an extent, and that small lack of effort may be the difference between a B+ and an A-.

All that said, I keep in mind that **this is just one grade in one course.** This one grade needn't be any grandiose statement or my chance to make someone's day or teach him or her a lesson. It should be a fair and proper reflection of the work he or she did for the semester, and considered in that light, there is some wiggle room. In addition, there are many good reasons to grade "holistically" and not be married to your point totals, not the least of which is that assessing mastery is a tricky task and we must acknowledge that **the whole might indeed be greater than the sum of its parts.**

Many teachers get mired in the point totals. In our defense, it is simply easier and more consistent to stick to those points and not allow any wiggle room. But does that accumulation of points truly represent what that student leaves the class knowing about your subject? Each fall, I communicate to students that I grade holistically (meaning I do not rely solely on the rigid totaling of points; I look at their progress and overall level of mastery). However, (I tell them), they have to earn the points first. I will not, as a general rule, bump a student down in grade—only up—but such a measure is extremely rare and must be warranted.

I tell students that if they are teetering between two grades at the end of the semester (within a percentage point of the next level), I will first look to see if they turned in all their assignments. Did the grade matter to them? Did they make the effort to showcase their knowledge in every way possible? If the opportunities were there and they chose not to take advantage of them, I am certainly not going to do it for them. But if they've turned in every assignment, I consider how deep their understanding of the content was. For chemistry, this means lab reports and test grades. For English, it might mean overall writing skill and important essays. Does their performance on these tasks make them worthy of a grade boost? If one or both of these are strong, and they simply struggle with test anxiety or are still working on their writing skills, I judge whether the grade will still properly reflect their knowledge of the subject if I forgive them these difficulties and bump the grade.

Remember that I try not to take myself or my job too seriously. I try to be generous, keeping in mind that I don't want to set a precedent that grades can change often or without due justification. **Most important is that I am able to justify any grading decision I make, even to parents of *other* students**, since they may well hear through the grapevine that "Casey's grade went up, so why not Jamie's?" Check your own motivations here and make sure you are not falling prey to biases or other influences, and then do what feels right.

JOB 6: GO HOME HAPPY

"They Go Home Tired. You Go Home."

You may have heard this expression. I keep it handy and remind myself of it often. The students are the ones who need to learn the material, so

> **They go home tired.**
> **You go home.**

they are the ones who should be working the hardest, not you. **Ironically, often the students who do the least create the most work for you.** These unmotivated students require the most help and encouragement, your best effort at creating engaging lessons, and a higher level of vigilance and communication, from following up on assignments with them and providing after-school help to behavior management and prompt contact with parents and counselors. So **catch yourself when your efforts are disproportionate to theirs,** and remember that you can and should lead the horse to water, but you can't always make it drink. Do all you can for that student, but check that it is within reason and proportional to the response you are getting back.

Expect the Best

In the big scheme of things, **the content you're teaching isn't so important, but the interactions you have with your students and the life skills you teach them are.** Do you truly still remember all your Spanish vocabulary, the difference between meiosis and mitosis, the dates of each of the critical battles in World War I, the formula for the volume of a circle? Probably not, but hopefully you have internalized the *skills* you used to learn those details and the work habits it took to apply them. What you probably remember best are the teachers who got you excited, encouraged you, helped you improve, and left you feeling empowered and capable. So expect the best from yourself and work hard for your students, but also remember that this is one small part of their day and their lives, and that **a kind word and a friendly face may be something they need much more than any concept you are trying to teach**.

Also expect—and look for—the best in every student. You now have an arsenal of strategies at the ready for your students. Some will struggle and resist the learning opportunities you give them. If that gets you down, remember that the Pygmalion effect has been verified many times. Expecting and believing that your students are capable and can be successful helps them become so. As we've all seen, when kids are held to high standards, they may grumble and complain, but they can't help but take it as a compliment, because it means you know they are capable of more. So believe your students can be successful, and they will be.

ACKNOWLEDGMENTS

As you now know, I steal every good idea I can find, so I don't pretend for a moment that the ones shared here are all my own. Most, if not all, were adapted or reworked from others. I've given acknowledgment where I can, but the flow of information from classroom to classroom is great, so attributing ideas to the original source is not easy. Let it suffice to say that I am forever grateful to all those teachers whose ingenuity and creativity have reached me and my students. You've come up with some great stuff.

Thank you, specifically, to my mentor and friend, Millard Neymark, for showing me what a true science classroom looks like. To my cooperating teacher, Paul Koenig, a master of sports, science, and song, I salute you. A big thank you to David Kranz and David Strick for introducing me to keepers like Contract Projects, the Rocks and Minerals Dichotomous Key, and Plate Tectonics Land.

To Andy Arner, who could make any math topic fun, I still wear my Math Invaders T-shirt in your honor and think of you during every game of Math Mania. Cheers to Tom Walsh, for being my champion, teaching me to write proper objectives, and allowing me to benefit from his years of experience. To my friend and colleague Heather Lattimer, thank you for your professional guidance and for setting the bar so high. And to Steve Holstrom—for his multiple rounds of edits and advice— are we even yet? Finally, a much belated and unctuous bow to Benjamin Mahle and Good Apple Publishing for *Power Teaching*, the book that was most helpful to me starting out.

To my parents: thank you, Craige, for helping me do-be-have (yes, that's what I meant). To my most enthusiastic editor, my mother, thank you for cleaning up after me once again. To my girls, a giant monkey hug for teaching me how to parent, for accommodating my strange work hours, and for cleaning up after yourselves. Finally, to my husband, Chris, for your uncanny willingness to support me in any endeavor, however outlandish, I owe you yet again. Thanks for putting up with me and helping me to cultivate some patience, a little sass, and—when necessary—my indifference.

www.ingramcontent.com/pod-product-compliance
Lightning Source LLC
Chambersburg PA
CBHW071600040426
42452CB00008B/1238